How Republicans can WIN
in a changing America:

The art of war with lesson plans

by:

S. J. Helgesen and V. Lance Tarrance

1

How Republicans can win in a changing America

FORWARD

George W. Bush almost got it right when he tried his hand at the old Italian proverb: "When a man deceives me once shame on him; if twice shame on me." Truer words were never spoken, especially when applied to the victims of American political hyperbole and the empty promises of the 2008 and 2012 campaigns of President Barack Obama.

Since the Republicans' narrow (52% to 48%) defeat - for the second time - at the hands of the Obama juggernaut in November of 2012, many professional cynics have already ordered the headstone and written the epitaph for the Republican Party.

Indeed, after suggesting that the Rs fold up their small exclusive tent and make apologies to their die-hard base for their shellacking at the polls, pundits are encouraging the Republicans to take the long march to the history books, because "they clearly have no place in the world of *new* American politics."

America needs two political parties that are willing to exercise serious and respectful political discourse in an open marketplace of ideas and opinion. Our democracy is not well-served by any party that believes that a 52% majority is sufficient justification for thrusting a hot poker in the eyes of the opposition and expecting them to say "thank you sir, may I have another."

The truth is we do need each other and we also need to return to civility. Though the road to civility may be overgrown and barely recognizable, Republicans have a duty to clear it of vitriol and pettiness. This book is not an apology, a collection of excuses for Republicans' loss in 2012, an attack on the Democratic Party as such, or an academic treatise.

How Republicans can win in a changing America

It is, instead, a Republican <u>call to action.</u>

By looking back and examining voter demographics and voting patterns between the two major generational political Presidential elections (1980 and 2012), we offer the reader cold hard analysis *and a plan* for achieving Republican victories in the upcoming Congressional elections of 2014 and the Presidential election in 2016.

Our book is a resounding rejection and repudiation of nay-saying political prognosticators who are intent on administering the last rites to the Republican Party.

It is neither the *Little Red Book* of Mao nor the *Rules for Radicals* by Saul Alinsky that were designed to bring <u>down</u> systems. Ours celebrates the nation's founding principles which were forged from the crucible of human trials and tribulations and protected for over two centuries by patriots on and off the battlefield.

We offer insight on what happened to American society since the Reagan election of 1980 up to the present day's left-wing swing of Obama 2.0. We believe that it is time for a less *perfect* ideology and instead more common sense and uncommon courage for today's and tomorrow's Republican leaders.

Most importantly, we offer a realistic vision for a renewed and vibrant Republican Party AND a blueprint for its future success.

CONTENTS

How Republicans can win in a changing America

ACKNOWLEDGEMENTS

I wish to thank my parents, Mary and Lance Sr., for their unfailing support and inspiration over the course of my life and to the following people for their kindness and counsel: Roger Ailes, Charlie Black, Ray Bliss, Bill Clements, Jim Clifton, Charlie Cook, Walter DeVries, Bob Goodman, Peter O'Donnell, Jim Reese, Thom Rielly, Ken Rietz and Senators Pete Domenici, Phil Gramm and John Tower.

V. Lance Tarrance

Without the encouragement and extraordinary patience of my parents: Walter and Barbara, to keep asking questions, I would have simply accepted the world as it is instead of trying to improve it. For that, I am truly grateful.

S. J. Helgesen

How Republicans can win in a changing America

DEDICATION

We dedicate this book to America's Founding Fathers, the framers of our Constitution and Bill of Rights without whom we would still be drinking overtaxed tea and bemoaning our lack of liberty. We also dedicate this book to all future Republican candidates who will, one day, dare to leave the safety of their comfort zones and stand up for our precious American values. We urge them to reset our dreams by **R**e-invigorating the **R**epublican Party. Now is the time to **R**edouble our efforts and **R**enew our faith in each other. It is never too late to do the **R**ight thing...or choose the **R**ight path.

INTRODUCTION

We have chosen to divide our book into two distinct sections. The first is a brief look back in time at two seminal elections in American history: the 1980 election that gave us the *Reagan Revolution* and that of 2012 that gave President Barack Obama another term to drive his liberal ideology home. We believe that each was a watershed moment in our political evolution that moved us to this point in time of near total, self-imposed, ideological apartheid.

The second section is a call to action to all conservatives and guardians of the Constitution to redouble their efforts to restore the core values of personal responsibility, fidelity to the law, freedom from unnecessary legislation and a rejection of the Government's overreach and intrusion into our personal lives.

Unlike the current administration in Washington, we do not encourage further estrangement and division among Americans. We support a uniting of Americans around our founding principles.

We encourage respect for the individual, an appreciation of a strong national conscience, political cooperation and compromise but without capitulation. We stand for a resurgence of intense and steadfast involvement within the Republican Party by its members.

We advocate a reformation of the Party through an open and ongoing dialogue among its many factions. We support a rededication to inclusiveness and a renewal of our commitment to attract new members who will devote themselves to strengthening and expanding the Party's reach into all ethnic communities and with persons of diverse backgrounds.

How Republicans can win in a changing America

While our beliefs are strongly Republican in nature, they are, essentially, American in character.

Translated, that means that we believe in the rights and responsibilities of the individual, the right of the majority to govern and the viability of the two-party system. We are not prepared to surrender to a future of perpetual political gridlock or administrations that thumb their noses at the losers and adopt a *to the victor go the spoils* attitude.

We have chosen a direct first person narrative style and have used as few buzz words and clichés as possible. When actual quotes are offered they will be followed immediately in parentheses by the name of the person to whom they are attributed, instead of in footnotes.

While our message is an inclusive one for both men and women, we have opted to use the male pronoun when referring to individuals only because there is not yet a universally acceptable general pronoun that can be used for both men and women (we find his/hers, she/he and him/her too clumsy).

Finally, we thank you for buying this book and sincerely hope that you will answer its call to action. Our country needs you.

The Authors

P.S. For those of you who may be interested in what the R^2 pin on the cover of this book symbolizes, it stands for a re-doubling of Republicans' efforts to win in future elections. Individual pins or bulk orders (for Republican fund-raising purposes) can be ordered from our website: www.howrepublicanscanwin.com

Chapter 1

The perfect storm
makes landfall

The center of the perfect storm sat smack in the Oval Office - a president who knew little or nothing about how America did business and who harbored a deep and abiding distrust of big corporations *except when they opened their wallets to his election campaign.*

Since taking office in 2009, Barack Obama has presided over the single most catastrophic economy in America's recent memory, and to the surprise of many, has had the temerity to make it worse with policies that even a first-year business school student would shun. So ingrained was his ignorance of business' role and its rightful place in American society that Barack Obama had the audacity to court its campaign contributions while ignoring its pleas for help.

To add insult to injury he proceeded to attack small businesses by accusing them of paying too little in taxes; told them that their success was not really theirs to boast about; and then saddled them with his signature 'Obamacare' law – a plan that would cause further irreparable damage to their bottom line. His hypocrisy knew no bounds as was evidenced by his appointment of General Electric CEO (and fellow Harvard alum) Jeffrey Immelt to head his Council of Economic Advisors.

This was not the GE of the fifties with Ronald Reagan as its spokesman who proudly stated the GE mantra, "Progress is our most important product." No, Immelt's GE paid zero corporate income tax in 2011, giving an entirely new meaning to the word *progress.* Cynics would call the Council pure window dressing, especially since it hadn't even met once during a six-month period leading up to the election. Small wonder that most American businesspeople were skeptical of any real positive change coming their way with role models like Immelt and the Council.

11

In the President's first term, his misguided ideologically-driven economic policies put the country in tremendous peril. The most significant of which was the $750 billion Economic Recovery and Reinvestment Act, aka, the *Stimulus Package* which doled out free money for dubious projects as fast as the Treasury could print it!

Instead of creating new jobs, much of the stimulus money went to pay the salaries of hundreds of thousands of already-employed state workers.

Republican strategists regarded Obama's mismanagement of the economy as a gift served up on a silver platter, the perfect target for their eventual nominee, former Massachusetts Governor and America's turnaround specialist, Willard (Mitt) Romney. After all, this was a man who survived an interminably long primary process that left nearly all the Republican candidates bloodied from too many debates. Surely he could take the fight to Obama.

As the last man standing, Romney's task was not only to convince the opposition that he was the right man for the job, but also court the *hesitant ones* in his own party who remained cool to his impeccable resumé, cheerful countenance, picture-perfect family, wealth and above all else, smarts.

Despite their misgivings, most Republicans were psyched and energized and outwardly pleased to have a candidate they perceived as a smidgeon more to the right than their standard-bearer in 2008, Senator John McCain. They were finally going to take down the man some in the conservative news media called the *Messiah* or the *Anointed One* with their own version of the *Terminator*. But they forgot one small thing...

How Republicans can win in a changing America

Barack Obama was a seasoned community organizer and activist, and he knew the streets well. He also knew how to play the game and get his movement and ideas funded. AND he was the incumbent.

After enduring months of whistle-stops, town hall meetings and rope lines, both candidates squared off in three face-to-face Presidential debates.

Romney acquitted himself well in debate number one. After a weak showing in number two, the President bounced back with a vengeance in number three and subsequently painted Romney as a Wall Street *vampire*, out of touch with real America, thereby reinforcing the evil-doer persona invented by his advisors. Then he deftly passed the baton to his surrogates and his crack troops on the ground to fight the dirty war in the trenches while he happily flashed his winning smile for the whirring cameras in numerous softball interviews with the mainstream media.

Several things happened that prevented Romney from taking the brass ring of the Presidency.

The most important one was, undoubtedly, *The Machine* (the Obama campaign). It was a well-oiled, field-tested, efficient collection of thousands of volunteers and paid staffers, whose only purpose in life was to get Barack Obama re-elected. This machine resembled a high-tech kitchen appliance that could slice, dice, chop, crush, pulverize and liquefy any and all chances the Rs might have (or thought they might have) of winning.

Second, but by no means subordinate to the importance of The Machine, was the failure of candidate Romney's own campaign which, according to some, "held him back and kept him on a leash of civility" and in general made it a foregone conclusion

13

that this nice guy would certainly finish last. Ironically, it may have been Romney's pleasant nature and respectful demeanor as well as more than a few political gaffes, combined with The Machine that cost him the election.

On November 6th, the President got 303 electoral votes and four more years at 1600 Pennsylvania Avenue. The Mayflower Movers could sleep in. No one was going anywhere until January 2017. This was a game-changing or game-solidifying election perhaps more than any in recent memory (except for Mr. Obama's first election to the Presidency in 2008) because it revealed certain undeniable truths about how American politics is now being conducted in the new post-civility age.

The election also laid bare the glaring weaknesses and vulnerability of the Republican Party, its failure to accurately assess the mood of the electorate AND its gross underestimation of the strength of the Democrats and their ability to organize their troops. Practicing Republicans will tell you that this election hurt more than most because so much was riding on it: economic prosperity and debt reduction, job creation, Obamacare, immigration reform, Supreme Court Justice appointments, etc.

Since their defeat in 2012, many Rs still live in the land of denial. Others walk around in a stupor, repeatedly shaking their heads in disbelief at what comes out of the White House Press Room on an almost daily basis. A third group is just plain angry and wants to get even.

But there is a fourth group.

They are the committed realists of the Party - older, wiser, experienced hands who've seen victory and defeat up close and who know that 'every dog has his day.'

How Republicans can win in a changing America

They know, too, that along with the spoils of victory go the enormous challenges of governing a country in flux and that governance often presents exploitable opportunities for the opposing forces. This group is made up of people from literally every wing of the Party.

They are united in their belief that everyone benefits from a smaller and more responsive government that is faithful to the process and the people. It is the only government America truly deserves.

The U.S. electorate is, indeed, at a tipping point that will decide whether expansive government or more limited government is the right course. The question this book will deal with is, "Can Republicans win future elections without turning themselves into a patchwork policy Frankenstein or one that betrays its core values?"

We believe the answers are all around us, but without a serious Party-wide dialogue and commitment to change they are like so many trees that fall in the forest without an audience.

They will not be heard nor will they matter.

Chapter 2

Measuring generational change: America in 1980

Think back to the *good old days* of 1980.

Our country was suffering from a severe case of emotional and economic depression. We were even reminded of it (as if it were really necessary) by a President who used a *Misery Index* to measure it and who, ironically, ended his presidency with the highest score of misery for any President to date.

Jimmy Carter was no Jiminy Cricket. His conscience could rarely be seen or even felt, so detached was this President from the realities that beset the America of the late 1970s. The world seemed to be falling apart and this CEO was seen to be AWOL.

Our years-long oil crisis appeared to be coming to an end, but the taking of 52 American hostages in November of 1979 by a rogue government in Iran was a painful reminder that we were neither out of the energy 'woods' nor were we any longer the unassailable toughest kid on the international block.

In 1980, our population was 226,545,805 of whom 164,597,000 were eligible to vote. Registered voters accounted for 113,043,734. Only 86,515,221 of them actually voted. Baby boomers were into their fourth decade of life, and the number of people 55 or over was 47,253,000 of whom 26,796,000 were women and 20,458,000 were men. Of the total population, Caucasians (Whites) accounted for 83.4% or 189,035,012; African Americans (Blacks) were 11.7% or 26,482,349; Hispanics were 6.4% or 14,603,683 and Asians were 1.6% or 3,726,440.

Our average income was around $19K/year. The minimum wage was $3.10/hour. Our national debt was $914 billion. The average cost of a home was $68K. The average rental was $300/month. A new car cost about $8K. A gallon of gas cost $1.19. A loaf of bread was about 50 cents; a pound of ground beef was $1.00. Our national unemployment rate was 7.5%.

There were about 1.3 million abortions done in the U.S. in 1980 along with 2.4 million marriages and 1.2 million divorces. Our life expectancy was 77 years for women and 70 years for men. Our Congress had 277 Democrat representatives and 158 Republicans. Our Senate was comprised of 58 Democrats and 42 Republicans.

The most popular TV shows were Dallas, Three's Company, MASH and the Love Boat. We watched between 12-15 hours of television per week per person. Twenty million people a week went to the movies and saw The Empire Strikes Back, Raging Bull and Friday the 13th. CNN started operations in 1980. America was only computerized at the scientific level, and the public Internet didn't really exist for all intents and purposes.

Cellular phones were as big as thermos bottles. We had no electronic social media. We bade farewell to our eight track tapes and embraced cassette tapes as the audio recording medium of choice. GM reported its first loss since 1921. Israel and Egypt traded Ambassadors for the first time. Mount St. Helens erupted. There were 80 million households, and 62 million of them got a daily or Sunday newspaper.

While statistics don't lie, they are really just a mark on the twine. They give us the results without much context. If you were 18 in 1980, you were probably partying at the disco rather than reading the Republican or Democratic Party platform. The generic nationwide newspaper, USA Today, was still two years away from being launched by Al Neuharth who died in April of 2013.

Neuharth was a trailblazer, a real newspaperman who challenged the dominance of big city newspapers like the 'Gray Lady' (the New York Times) and others as he pioneered the concept of the national newspaper. He was once quoted as

18

saying, "The First Amendment guarantees a free press. We in the media must make sure it is a fair press."

America's media in the 1980s was soon to undergo a sea change, but until then the traditional 'mainstream media' was still dominated by big city newspapers and the big three television networks. Local newspapers were still making a profit delivering local news and the networks were still capturing the big national advertising dollar while enjoying a collective reputation as 'serious' and 'credible' sources for news.

Americans were weary of political spin even back then, but those who were interested in separating fact from fiction knew there weren't many places to get their information. We all fed from the same trough and had to sort it out as best as we could.

The Internet was still a ways off and *blogs*, *bloggers* and *blogging* weren't even words in our lexicon. Political commentators in the print media still had sway and continued to poke fun (sometimes not so good-naturedly) at every politician who puffed up his feathers and 'bloviated' (thanks to Bill O'Reilly for that one).

Our nation was on the verge of a Republican Renaissance, but we wouldn't know that until November when a Hollywood actor named Ronald Reagan would become the 40th President of these United States. In the meantime, we went about our work (or tried to find work as our unemployment reached epidemic proportions).

We bought 'muscle cars' like the Z28 Camaro and the first SUV (the 'Eagle' by American Motors). We couldn't get enough of the Japanese models either. In 1979, OPEC tripled the price of a barrel of oil, and in 1980 we suffered with $1.40/gallon gas. This didn't bode well for the gas guzzlers we had grown up with and

19

spiked interest for more miserly gas consuming vehicles, hence the demand for Japanese cars.

This was just six months before the Japanese government (on the insistence of the U.S. government) organized a cartel for the export of vehicles to the U.S. and instituted a VER (Voluntary Export Restraint) on its automakers, designed to halt the flood of Japanese exports so we in the U.S. had time to catch up. The VER would last for seven years, but it did little to curb long-term demand.

In 1980, McDonalds posted sales of $6.2 billion (in 2012 the figure was $6.9 billion), and if we are truly what we eat then we were all fast fooders in 1980. According to the USDA, the number of fast food outlets increased from 30,000 in 1970 to 140,000 in 1980, and fast food sales increased by about 300% over the same period. Market share was the brass ring, and in the coming years, American fast food giants would be slugging it out in an all out 'burger war.'

Microsoft ended 1980, the same year Steve Ballmer joined the company, with sales of $8 million with 40 employees. *(In 2012, the company's revenue, operating income and earnings per share were: $72.7 billion, $21.8 billion and $2 per share.)* Not to be outdone, Apple went public with 4.6 million shares, the largest offering since Ford Motor Company went public in 1956.

America's amusement park, Disneyland, turned 25 and attracted nearly 200 million visitors to its California facility. America's gambling Mecca, Las Vegas, was busy building new theme hotels/casinos. Circus Circus celebrated its fourth birthday in 1980, the same year that nearly 12 million people visited this playful oasis in the desert.

In the latter part of the 80s, Las Vegas would see competition from other states who would dip their toes in the lucrative waters of the gambling industry, but in 1980 things looked good for them as Americans tried to forget their daily troubles.

The year and the Presidential campaigns eventually wound down and ended with perhaps one of the most famous quotes ever uttered by a candidate for the country's highest office. On October 28th, at the Presidential Debate in Cleveland's Convention Center, Ronald Reagan turned to Jimmy Carter, and in his unmistakable, low, soft voice said, "There you go again." A week later, he became our 40th president.

Composition of the Electorate
1980 and 2012 Elections
Source: National election exit polls

ELECTION YEAR	1980	2012	+ or -
RACE			
Whites	89%	72%	- 17%
Blacks	10%	13%	+ 3%
Asians		3%	
Hispanics	1%	10%	+ 9%
GENDER			
Men	50%	47%	- 3%
Women	50%	53%	+ 3%
EDUCATION			
High School or less	41%	24%	- 17%
Some college	31%	29%	- 2%
College grad or Post grad	28%	47%	+ 19%
PARTY ID (self-described)			
Democrat	45%	38%	- 7%
Republican	30%	32%	+ 2%
Independent	26%	29%	+ 3%
RELIGION			
Protestant	51%	53%	+ 2%
Catholic	27%	25%	- 2%
Other			
None	6%	12%	+ 6%
UNION MEMBER HOUSEHOLDS	31%	18%	- 13%

22

Chapter 3

Measuring generational change:
America in 2012

In 2012, our population was 313 million.

Baby boomers were into their seventh decade and the number of people 55 or over was approximately 69 million, of which 34 million were women and 35 million, men.

The average home sale was $150,000 and average rents were $1,100. Our average income was $42,693 and the federally-mandated minimum wage was $7.25/hour. Our national debt was approaching $16 trillion. The average new car cost us $30K. A loaf of bread cost about $2.00, a pound of ground beef was about $4.75 and a gallon of gas was averaging $4.00. The unemployment rate was 7.8% for those who were still looking for work.

There were approximately 1.0 million abortions done in the U.S. in 2012 and approximately 2.0 million marriages along with approximately 800,000 divorces. Our life expectancy was 80 years for women and 75 years for men. The Senate had 51 Democrat senators after the 2012 elections and 47 Republicans. There were 201 Democrat House Representatives and 233 Republicans. The most popular TV shows were CSI, Dancing with the Stars, the Jon Stewart Show and the late night talk shows.

We watched an average of 28 hours of television per week per person. A whopping 1.36 billion movie theatre tickets were purchased in 2012 earning the studios $10.8 billion. Fox News celebrated its 16th year on cable and was rated "most trusted" by 34% of all American cable viewers. America was highly computerized and the Internet was an integral part of our daily lives. Electronic and social media was in full bloom with Facebook (1.1 billion users) and Twitter (554 million users).

Cellular phones were rapidly replacing landlines for personal use and small enough to fit into a shirt pocket. The newspaper penetration rate per household was dwindling. With over 120 million households, newspapers penetrated only 45 million of them.

Electronic downloads of music and films increased dramatically as the hardware available to play them became more sophisticated and pervasive (PDAs, PDA cellular phones and tablet computers). The success of cable TV channels outpaced traditional TV news programs. Hardcover books fell victim to electronic e-book readers and tablet computers, and the publishing industry was tightening its belt, bracing for its eventual demise. The Internet was rapidly becoming THE worldwide source for information and communication.

GM was moving through its bankruptcy after being bailed out by the U.S. taxpayer and the economy was still sputtering along trying to recover after four years of the worst recession since the Great Depression of the 1930s. The Middle East was in turmoil after experiencing the overthrow of governments from Egypt to Libya (with Syria teetering on all-out civil war and dissolution as of this writing). North Korea was threatening nuclear destruction while Iran worked feverishly to develop its own nuclear weapons of mass destruction.

The day before Election Day...

Americans were primed and ready for the election booth. Both Republicans and Democrats were confident that their candidate would be victorious. After four tumultuous years of sky-high unemployment and after failing to turn around an anemic economy with two failed expensive stimulus attempts (TARP and ARRA), the Obama Administration kept the pressure on the rich to pay their *fair share* and effectively presented them as a

25

straw man for the Democrats' voter base to hate. This was not unexpected, especially when considering the Administration's track record of attempting to divide America along gender, racial, economic and ideological lines since 2008. It is widely believed that the *War on Women* the Democrats accused the Republicans of waging, won over a substantial number of young women to the Ds' side.

For the Republicans, their primary debates may have served to split the less faithful from the more ideologically pure candidates, and the Party shot itself in the foot by holding way too many of them.

The Democrats couldn't have been more pleased as this gave them a target rich environment from which they could attack the front runners and point to Republican disunity and/or 'extremism.' The absence of a Democratic competitor to the President helped the Dems focus their resources on getting their man elected, and they used those resources well.

Democrat surrogates, PAC representatives, campaign workers and the mainstream media rallied around Barack Obama. Team Obama virtually ignored the dismal economy and instead used a diversionary tactic by demonizing the Republican Party and focused on the destruction of the Republican candidate just as Jimmy Carter attempted to do in 1980.

The Rs also did their share of hammering away at the opposition and the President's AWOL-like mismanagement of the national economy. Unfortunately, they had to spend an inordinate amount of time repelling attacks on Governor Romney's personal wealth and deflecting the corporate raider/looter label that the Ds tried to pin on him.

How Republicans can win in a changing America

In short, the America of November 6th was so politically divided it was difficult to detect any middle ground. It was ready for a political high colonic.

With all this, the 44th President was elected to a second term.

Why?

Like the election of 1876, when voter participation was 81.8% with an electorate made up mostly of white males, the election of 2012 was also comprised mostly of white males. Even though the participation rate was 20 percentage points smaller, it was still the third largest since the election of 1960 that saw John Kennedy win the Presidency.

But that's where the similarity ends.

Election 2012 saw a swelling of the numbers of women (young and old single and married) supporting Mr. Obama over Mitt Romney: single women 67% and married women 48%. Hispanics/Latinos supported him by 71% over Romney. The President's most loyal group, African Americans/Blacks ended up giving him all of their votes (93%).

Geographically, both coasts with their liberal/progressive populations supported the President as did the Midwestern states of Illinois, Wisconsin and Minnesota. The Mid-Atlantic States, the South and much of the West stuck with Governor Romney, but the great spoiler, the Electoral College, swept away any hopes of a Romney win like Legionnaire's disease in a crowded hospital ward.

Question: Who really elected Barack Obama or at least pushed him over the top?

How Republicans can win in a changing America

Answer: Single women and minorities...AND stay-at-home Republicans.

To understand why these demographic groups voted with the Democrats, we must first acknowledge something right from the start: America has changed mightily since 1980.

Ozzie and Harriet are dead. The Beaver is in his sixties and the miserly Prius has replaced the muscle cars of the past.

We're no longer a nation of suburbanite Whites with a smattering of non-White homeowners stuck in the far corners of the subdivision. Many of our inner cities now have disproportionately large numbers of minority voters: Black and/or Hispanic and Asian. The bankrupt city of Detroit, for example, has a Black population that has now surpassed 80%.

Voter registration (Get Out The Vote or GOTV) drives were successfully undertaken by the Democrats in these heavily minority-populated inner city neighborhoods and on college campuses. Those drives brought hundreds of thousands of new voters onto the rolls, but many of these voters had little in common with the politics, attitudes or values of your father or grandfather.

Instead, they're a broad mix of socio-economic and ethnic groups encompassing large numbers of the unemployed, single mothers and often the socially poor with lower to mixed educational levels. The younger (under 25) voters like the Internet, rap music, 'Dancing with the Stars,' tattoos, iphones, You Tube, Twitter and Facebook. They believe the U.S. Government is just another service-provider like their mobile phone company and are quick to demand their rights from the system.

How Republicans can win in a changing America

They join groups that are hip like Occupy Wall Street and look down on groups like the Tea Party because they are composed of older 'out-of-touch' adults. Many are approaching their mid-twenties owing a ton of money for college loans, and while a sizable percentage of them don't have jobs or can even fathom the prospect of finding one anytime soon, they see the government as a battering ram to help break down the *barriers* to their entry into the workforce AND provide for them while they wait for it to happen.

Question: Why did these young people vote for Obama?

Answer: He's youthful in appearance, cool, slim, smiles a lot, talks their talk, plays basketball, tried drugs and appears to represent every progressive idea that young people usually hold dear like having unlimited freedom to do whatever they want, getting free contraceptives and healthcare to scoring low-cost college loans or loan forgiveness.

Add to that the President's love of sports, his cult-like celebrity status and his support for homosexual marriage and a 'pathway to citizenship' for the many millions of illegal immigrants in the country and you have THE perfect candidate for experience-challenged youth voters.

These are the hallmarks of the ideological bent of today's liberal youth whether they are on college campuses, at their parents' beach houses on the Hamptons or crowding Florida's beaches during Spring Break.

For them, Obama and the Democrats are the choice du jour like a latté with steamed milk at Starbucks. In fact, not voting for the Democrats is cause for banishment from the cool kids' crowd. You want to hang with Michele Bachmann or Michelle Obama?

Choosing the former will get you ostracized; the latter might get you a hot date with a hip college girl, especially if you're into exercise and healthy eating.

Understanding the single woman demographic is not the same as understanding the youth demographic, because while single college women might be lumped together with single college men for the purpose of analysis, non-college single women are more diverse in their opinions (as opposed to their older married sisters).

While they may want the same free stuff that their Sandra Flukean friends want like free contraceptives and abortion pills, they see the world differently - more idealistically (if not more emotionally) than their male counterparts.

Their social issues are: the *level playing field* including full pay parity with men, a harassment-free workplace (and world) and a president that espouses a no-war and no-gun platform, national healthcare, etc. They are not necessarily single-issue voters and are therefore more difficult to address and motivate with simple messages.

The Republicans have their work cut out for them if they expect to attract more of the young woman vote.

Chapter 4

New voter dynamics post-2012

A look at exit polls taken on Election Day 2012 revealed...

Hispanics are 17% of U.S. population now. In 2000, they were just 7% of the vote when 62% of them voted for the Democrats while only 35% voted for the Republicans. In 2012, they were 10% of the voting public (up 3%) when 71% of them voted for the Democrat candidate while only 27% of them voted for the Republican candidate.

African-Americans/Blacks are 12% of the U.S. population now. In 2000, they were 10% of the vote and voted 90% for the Democrats and just 9% voted for the Republicans. In 2012, they were 13% of the population (up 3%) and voted 93% for the Democrats.

Caucasians/Whites are 63% of the population now, and in the election of 2000, represented 81% of the vote when they voted 54% for the Republican candidate and 42% for the Democrat. In 2012, they represented 72% of the voters (down 9%) and voted 59% for the Republicans and 39% for the Democrats.

Single women are 26% of the U.S. population (age 15 and older) now, and in 2000 they were 19% of the vote when they voted 63% for the Democrats and 33% for the Republicans.

In 2012, they were 23% of the vote (up 4%) and voted 67% for the Democrats and 31% for the Republicans.

Married women (15 and older) are 25% of the U.S. population now. In 2000, they represented 33% of the vote when they voted 49% for the Republicans and 48% for the Democrats. In 2012, they represented 31% of the vote (down 2%) and voted 53% for the Republicans and 46% for the Democrats.

Caucasian/White men are 31% of the U.S. population now. In 2000, they represented 38% of the vote when they voted 60% for the Republicans and 36% for the Democrats. In 2012, their share of the vote was 34% (down 4%) when they voted 62% for the Republicans and 35% for the Democrats.

Caucasians/Whites without four-year college degrees (age 25 and older) represent 46% of the U.S. population now, and in 2000 voted 57% for the Republicans and 40% for the Democrats. Their share of the vote in 2012 was 36% (down 10%) when they voted 62% for the Republicans and 35% for the Democrats.

Sources: U.S. Census Bureau 2011 statistics and exit polls conducted for The Associated Press.

Crunch the numbers and the unmistakable conclusion you'll draw is that the Republicans lost because of: 1. a higher Democratic voter turnout, 2. a lower Republican voter turnout and 3. a higher percentage of Blacks, Hispanics and young women voting for the Democrats.

Had Mitt Romney received only 1.5 million more votes and Barack Obama received 2.0 million fewer the election would have gone the other way.

We must also understand that the election world today is much more complex and variegated. It is no longer simply, Republicans, Democrats, Independents and minorities. We believe that all campaign strategies will need to be more attentive and more nuanced to appeal to the ethnic voter, the low information voter, the emotional voter and many other potential single-issue voters. The colors of the campaign world today are much more than just Red, Blue and Purple.

The racial/ethnic voter

America's minority ethnic population is growing fast and with each passing year becomes more of a force in American politics. In 1980, self-identified Caucasians (Whites) represented 83.4% of the population. Non-whites comprised 16.6% of our country. As of the 2010 Census, Caucasians were at 72.4% with non-whites representing 27.6%. The fastest growing ethnic group was Hispanics, representing approximately 16.3% of the 2010 population, a whopping 43% growth since the 2000 census.

(Source: U.S. Census Bureau)

To make accurate generalizations about why the majority of them voted Democratic is nearly impossible, but every search for truth starts with a hypothesis.

One might be that Blacks and Hispanics voted for Obama because he was a minority (the 'One of Us' vote), and as such, their level of trust in his ability to watch their backs was higher than it was for the older, White, establishment candidate.

Another hypothesis might be that the campaign rhetoric of *fairness* and *equal and level playing field* resonated, especially among the lower socio-economic groups of ethnic voters (the 'Equality' vote). A third hypothesis is the simple Democrat vs. Republican choice among such groups ('The Common Man vs. the Rich Man vote') while a fourth could be based on real ideological differences that go beyond mere politics (the 'Enlightened' vote). Though there may be a smattering of each of those in the ethnic vote, it is incumbent upon Republicans to understand which of them was the dominant one if they are to successfully address these voters with messages that resonate <u>and</u> turn their votes from Blue to Red.

How Republicans can win in a changing America

Serious observers of the election cannot, however, honestly discount or dismiss the importance of the President's race or ethnicity to his win among these groups, but they should be intellectually curious enough to find other reasons for his victory among America's minorities as well.

The low/no information voter

A relatively new term was introduced into the popular parlance of the 2008/2012 elections, was that of the *low information voter* which accounts for about 30% of the U.S. voting age population. While some would say that this term is a euphemism for ignorant or lazy voter we'd prefer to use it to describe a person who is motivated to vote but who is ignorant, unaware or unconcerned about the issues and maybe even about the candidates, themselves.

This is not to say that low information voters are stupid and willfully ignore the issues. There may be many explanations for their largely uninformed status.

Some of them might be: "Politics is too complex and confusing; "I don't have the time to immerse myself in the issues"; "I trust my instincts to make good decisions" or "I don't trust the media to tell me the truth." Having only come into vogue these past few years, this group has actually been around forever.

Rarely, we believe, have these voters been as instrumental in the election of a president as they were in 2008 and 2012. Many low information voters are also *no information voters* and haven't even a passing acquaintance with the political issues of any given election. Their cluelessness often extends to lack of information about the candidates' political stance on key issues or their voting record.

35

This absence of information makes them an easy target for emotion-driven advertising, slogans and sound bites. They prove the point that a little information in the wrong hands can be a dangerous thing (especially for the candidate not engaging in populism).

Low information voters, like emotional or single-issue voters, can and do get swept up in the excitement of a campaign, and campaigns often use them to effectively buttress the ranks of other voters as long and do not expect them to move swiftly up the issue awareness curve.

The wise campaign will accept them for what they are. It will motivate them by recognizing their importance by appealing to their solidarity with the party and the candidate.

Some campaigns have inferred that, "it's not necessary to be an expert on the issues as long as we agree on the direction our candidate will take us" (something the Obama campaign did well).

The Obama campaign also gave them a mantra to chant (such as *'the rich man is bad because he is rich'*), and it gave them a reason to keep chanting it. Though it may be tempting to take this group for granted, a campaign does so at its own peril AND it must face one certainty...

Campaigns need the low information voter, and though there isn't enough time to bring them up to speed on issues before the election, they are important to the party because they will hopefully become the next generation of better informed voters over time. They are what they are, and their vote counts just as much as one from the *enlightened group* of voters.

How Republicans can win in a changing America

The emotional voter

Along with Reagan's "There you go again,""I feel your pain" is probably one of the most memorable lines of any recent political campaign, and it was uttered by one of America's most silver-tongued door-to-door salesmen, President William Jefferson Clinton, aka *Bubba*, the *Big Dog*. The line succeeded with emotional voters because the sentiments were actually felt (or gave the impression they were felt) by Mr. Clinton, himself.

Because of his ability to convey this earnestness to people on the campaign trail, he won over their emotions. The emotional voter wants to be in love with the candidate, his ideals and words. This is not to say, however, that the emotional voter is a one trick pony and doesn't understand the issues of the campaign. It just underscores the important part human emotions play in choosing which candidate to support.

Many emotional voters are willing to project themselves and their aspirations onto a candidate that best represents their own philosophy, AND they're willing to make the emotional investment necessary to stand by that candidate. The emotional voter is not necessarily a fickle voter and will show his fidelity to his candidate even in the most trying of times (take the various women scandals of the aforementioned Bill Clinton, for example).

To desert a candidate would be like admitting a serious error in one's own judgment in choosing that candidate, and no emotional voter wants to think of himself as a poor judge of character. Without putting too fine a point on it, emotional voters are passionate people, but they can be easily seduced by a candidate that exudes the right mixture of charm, friendliness, rhetoric and yes, even sex appeal.

37

Every campaign needs its emotional voters for they are the ones that pack the seats at town hall meetings, the bleachers at state and county fairs and populate countless other whistle-stop venues. They are the first string cheerleaders that chant and swoon and inspire the lesser emotional voters to join them in rousing rounds of applause.

The quid pro quo voter

As the name implies, this voter may or may not have an ideological preference but does vote for the candidate he believes will deliver on a specific campaign promise, usually something tangible that will improve their lives like expanded entitlement programs. It is widely believed, that in the 2012 election, millions of voters were quid pro quo voters, casting their ballots on the basis of pragmatism and to a lesser degree, a deep-rooted political ideology.

In short, they voted to keep President Obama in office so that he could deliver on promises to dramatically change society...for them.

Some of those changes were: to make homosexual marriage the law of the land, to regularize the status of illegal immigrants and provide them with a 'pathway to citizenship' (many Republicans believe this is code for a general amnesty), free contraception and free abortion (including late term abortion), a retreat from 'nation-building' and the world stage as it relates to our military commitments. Others were: carbon taxes and environmental remediation, expanded alternative energy, higher taxes on the evil rich, expansion of entitlements, tightened gun control laws, cheap or no-cost college tuitions and college loan forgiveness and more rather than less federal regulation, thus consolidating power at the federal level.

The quid pro quo voter is one of the most difficult to identify and analyze, and it is tempting to place all those voters who don't fit neatly into the other categories into this one. But that would be a mistake without serious attempts at polling or interviewing them. It would be unfair, for example, to lump all young, college-age women into such a category.

It might not be a stretch, however, to assume that of that very important voter demographic, a something-for-something attitude prevailed, due in part to the trumped-up *war on women* that the Democrats created out of thin air. It might be fair to posit that a significant percentage of Black voters supported the President out of a strong belief that he would heed their cries for help and do something about the 14% unemployment rate among Black adults and the nearly 70% rate among Black youth.

The single-issue voter

A cousin to the quid pro quo voter, this group shares their pragmatic approach to voting - to reap a return on their voting investment. However, the single-issue voter is more narrowly focused on achieving one particular objective while sacrificing or subordinating all the rest.

Putting it another way, these voters are willing to ignore a number of the candidate's other positions (on which they may disagree) as long as the candidate supports their single most important position - the one that has brought them to the Party or keeps them there.

These issues are all over the map and they include: abortion, homosexual marriage, government funded birth control, home schooling, gun control, expanding government budgets or fiscal responsibility, privacy issues, alternative energy vs. fossil fuels, the decriminalization of marijuana and other drugs, immigration

How Republicans can win in a changing America

policy, collective bargaining, election/campaign reform, healthcare, American adventurism abroad, the military industrial complex, mandatory sentencing/incarceration of criminals and law and order in general.

Both parties have expressed their official views on most of these issues through their party platforms and through the primaries and general election campaigns, so there should be little doubt in most single-issue voters' minds where the parties stand.

We believe that a single-issue voter is also a bundler of issues, and that even though their support for their chosen issue will influence which candidate they will vote for, it will not sway them from sticking with the party that best speaks to their general mindset or how they view the world.

For example, a staunch supporter of *abortion on demand* will most likely vote Democratic as his overarching view on society in general is defined by his support for freedom of choice.

Translated, that means he shares the relativist view of the Democratic Party on these matters (the mother chooses) rather than the absolutist view of the Republicans (all life must be protected). Other examples, like comprehensive immigration reform, also serve to smoke out the party preference of the single-issue voter. If they advocate reform that views the illegal immigrant as a victim and the act of illegal border crossing to escape a failed state as a necessity (and not a crime) then the single-issue voter will, in all likelihood, vote Democratic.

Those who wish meaningful reform and would support strict adherence to the letter of the law and a demonstrable tightening of border controls and improved surveillance would probably vote Republican.

We believe that the major differences between Democrat and Republican single-issue voters are rooted in an overarching attitude of relativism or absolutism. The bottom line is that, absent any specific data, the relativist or absolutist argument is a fairly reliable predictor of how people will vote.

The independent/non-aligned voter

There are many political pundits who believe that there is much less independence and much more commonality among independent and non-aligned voters than is generally thought. Americans have always prided themselves on being independent, and who could blame any voter for not wanting to identify himself too closely with either party these days, especially if you believe the 14% approval rating of the House and Senate?

Still, campaigns continue to court these voters and attempt to woo them over to their side in the hopes that they will somehow make the critical statistical difference and push their candidate over the top. In 22 states, registered Independent voters may not participate in either Democratic or Republican primaries and are, therefore, effectively disenfranchised from choosing candidates for the general election.

That is a bridge too far for many voters, which is why they 'hold their noses' and register as a member of one of the two major parties. Many Independents, however, are willing to stand on the sidelines while their neighbors decide who will enter the political ring for the final face-off.

We believe that most Independent voters philosophically favor one of the two major political parties, and that regardless of how much attention is paid to them, they will cast their votes according to their core preference.

41

Future campaigns should consider spending less money on trying to persuade this group to cross over and instead simply accept that they will vote along the same lines as *regular* voters.

The enlightened voter

The enlightened voter is the gold standard of voter groups and accounts for about 25-30% of all voters. The group is comprised of knowledgeable issue-savvy voters who have formed their political beliefs and come to their ideological conclusions over the course of many years. This is the bedrock of each party's base and one that won't switch its allegiance unless a major shift has occurred in the party platform.

True enlightened voters track the candidates' movements and follow their decisions, carefully, and are the ones who vote in primaries, attend town halls and write to their Congressmen.

In addition, they religiously monitor candidates' speeches and will, whenever necessary, be openly and vocally critical of them. Enlightened voters regard themselves as the party faithful and the party's standard bearers. They are often looked up to (but ironically also taken for granted) by leaders in the party hierarchy.

The problem is that this group is roughly the same size in both parties, and their votes tend to cancel out each other's. As we've seen, there are many different types of voters, and in the last election, the Democrats changed their strategy to pick them off, very carefully, with individual approaches.

Instead of only appealing to the voters 'above the line' (the elitist party-faithful voter), they played a different game and dipped 'below the line' to those who were the uninformed, no/low information voter and traditional non-participant.

How Republicans can win in a changing America

Most elections are played out with about 75-80% of the registered voters (those 'above the line') who tend to be very attentive, ideological, and extremely partisan. It's hard to convert or capture these votes because the group has already made up its mind.

They represent approximately 30% of the total registered voters. The second group above the line represents about 40-45% of all voters. They are ones who don't pay much attention to elections, will not consume the same cost, but in the final analysis will still vote.

The elections of the recent past (10 years or so) have been won by appealing to that 75-80% of total registered voters, but these elections have been very narrow. Republicans won a lot of Congressional and Senatorial elections during the 'Bush years' but they won them narrowly. Since then, they've been *losing* narrowly. In 2012, the Rs lost five key swing states.

Republicans have been understandably confused about this. They now know that the mix of political participants has changed and that the Dems changed up their tactics and went after the low information voter and the non-participant to get their majority. Now, instead of 75% or 80% of the electorate making the decision, it's closer to 85%. Some shifted down; some shifted up.

The Obama campaign pulled from the 40% below the line. The group listened to him, believed his promises and voted for him. This is how Obama surprised so many pundits and so many polls. If Republicans want to win in 2014 and 2016 they had better look below the line or they'll find themselves on the losing end, again.

How Republicans can win in a changing America

Composition of the Electorate
1980 and 2012 Elections
Source: National election exit polls

ELECTION YEAR	<u>1980</u>	<u>2012</u>	<u>+ or -</u>
RACE			
Whites	89%	72%	- 17%
Blacks	10%	13%	+ 3%
Asians		3%	
Hispanics	1%	10%	+ 9%
GENDER			
Men	50%	47%	- 3%
Women	50%	53%	+ 3%
EDUCATION			
High School or less	41%	24%	- 17%
Some college	31%	29%	- 2%
College grad or Post grad	28%	47%	+ 19%
PARTY ID (self-described)			
Democrat	45%	38%	- 7%
Republican	30%	32%	+ 2%
Independent	26%	29%	+ 3%
RELIGION			
Protestant	51%	53%	+ 2%
Catholic	27%	25%	- 2%
Other			
None	6%	12%	+ 6%
UNION MEMBER HOUSEHOLDS	31%	18%	- 13%

How Republicans can win in a changing America

2012 Presidential Election Voting Results
Exit Poll
Source: CNNPolitics

Vote by Gender		Obama	Romney	+ or – Obama	
Men	- 47%	45%	52%	-	7%
Women	- 53%	55%	44%	+	11%

Vote by Age

		Obama	Romney	+ or – Obama	
18 -24 yrs old -	11%	60%	36%	+	24%
18-29 yrs old -	19%	60%	37%	+	23%
25-29 yrs old -	8%	60%	38%	+	22%
30-39 yrs old -	17%	55%	42%	+	13%
30-44 yrs old -	27%	52%	45%	+	7%
40-49 yrs old -	20%	48%	50%	-	2%
45-64 yrs old -	38%	47%	51%	-	4%
50-64 yrs old -	28%	47%	52%	-	5%
65 and older -	16%	44%	56%	-	12%

Vote by Race

		Obama	Romney	+ or – Obama	
White -	72%	39%	59%	-	20%
Black -	13%	93%	0%	+	93%
Latino -	10%	71%	27%	+	44%
Asian -	3%				

Chapter 5

Predicting the future:
The pundit and pollster industry

"If you are not in a position to shape the future...

then you might as well try to predict it" is something only detractors of polling organizations might say when asked about the importance of modern-day voter polling. While that might make for a good sound bite for someone looking to downplay the importance of polling it's way off the mark.

The truth is that the industry has grown wiser and more relevant with the advent of sophisticated polling techniques, computer modeling and analysis. In fact, the leaders in the business (Gallup, Rasmussen, the Pew Research Center, etc.) have now been joined by smaller *boutique* organizations affiliated with think tanks, universities and the networks.

It's quite normal that every political organization is firmly focused on the future and wants to be the first and most accurate with its predictions while relegating analysis of the past to the back seat.

To those who would ignore the important research and analysis being done on past elections we offer a quote from Yogi Berra, "The future aint what it used to be."

Staying with the future for awhile, one of the more interesting aspects of professional polling is the focus group, a fairly accurate method of testing advertising slogans and for determining the receptiveness of consumers to new products AND candidates. The focus groups of Frank Luntz (Luntz Global) have become good television for Fox News, but the company is not Fox's handmaiden. Luntz takes great pains to assemble politically-balanced audiences for airing on the Sean Hannity Show, for example.

He then gives them the 'dials' (the interactive electronic apparatus subjects use to indicate their agreement or disagreement, pleasure or displeasure at commercials or speeches) and shows them topical material generated by candidates, their surrogates or their campaigns.

Admittedly, focus groups make for better television than a polling company representative with a sheaf of papers and a chalk board, but ask any political consultant about the importance of polling in general and he'll tell you that he couldn't do his job properly without it.

Do pollsters predict the future or make it?

The correct answer is a little bit of both. By identifying key voter groups and polling them regularly with topical questions, pollsters can see patterns and trends, which when combined with focus groups, more targeted interviewing and careful analysis, reveal a peek into the future, albeit through a thin veil of uncertainty.

Many Presidential elections ago, the major network news channels decided to stop airing the results of early exit polling and their subsequent analysis which led to 'calling' the state for this or that candidate. The reasoning was simple. They feared that this form of polling was actually influencing elections by encouraging voters to stay home and not vote. This gives some indication of how serious pollsters are regarded today.

Pundits are another story entirely. America has seen an explosion of professional and amateur political pundits (pundit: from the Hindi word, *pandit* meaning 1. a learned man, 2. teacher or 3. someone who gives opinions in an authoritative manner - a critic).

48

Every major news outlet, whether cable-based or traditional, has a stable of these characters it can call upon for pithy or controversial comments on every conceivable issue. Some are single-issue experts and some are political generalists. Either way, pundit proliferation has reached astronomical proportions.

In generations past, pundits were newspaper people, regular columnists - journalists with an edge. Some used humor, irony or satire to get their points across and some were just sensationalists.

The world of punditry changed with the advent of radio and television. Pundits became syndicated sages whose core political beliefs qualified them for seats at a network's 'ideology table,' from which they could reinforce the political line of the owners or operators. Then something happened that shook up the pundits. It was the Internet. Now pundits have competition from the basement blogger and from successful opinion purveyors like the Huffington Post and Matt Drudge. On the plus side, they also have a medium to reach deeper into the minds of America's political junkies.

P.T. Barnum said, "A sucker is born every minute," but in the world of the pundit there are no suckers, only uninformed and malleable readers/viewers that can be brought over to the pundit's network with a clever phrase and convincing viewpoint. That's entertainment, especially when the pundit club is expanded to include celebrities who have other day jobs like mayors, governors, senators, congressmen and former campaign managers and consultants.

The pundit 'tent' has gotten pretty crowded of late, so much so, that it's hard to tell the players without a scorecard, but it's not usually hard to identify their political ideology.

If you're on CNN regularly you're probably left of center; MSNBC, ultra left, PBS, left of center to Progressive, Fox News, center to right and mixed, and on the 'mainstream media' TV you are left of center. Punditry is pervasive, and when mixed with polling, rounds out the 'meal' served up to inform, entertain and sometimes enlighten American voters.

Chapter 6

Measuring generational change:
A life's work

Not many boys dream of becoming scientific pollsters.

And neither did Lance Tarrance. Polling was an emerging science in the early 50s and there wasn't an army of people doing it, either. Growing up in Texas, my interests were much like everyone else's. I wasn't particularly taken with politics and could barely name one Senator other than our own and maybe a couple Supreme Court Justices. It wasn't that I was ignorant. I just didn't care very much until somebody nominated me for class president in my senior year in high school.

The whole experience of campaigning was so foreign to me that I remember asking one of my friends, "Do you think I'll need to give speeches or make campaign promises?" Ah, those were the days of ignorant bliss. Turns out I won, and later in my college fraternity somebody threw my hat into the ring again. I guess I was either a good candidate or well-liked. I'd like to think both.

My head wasn't tuned to the political 'frequency' until much later when one day, nearing my graduation from Washington Lee University, a friend of mine who had already graduated handed me a pamphlet on Barry Goldwater. It was promoting his political philosophy and candidacy for the Republican Party's nomination for President and mentioned his book, "Conscience of a Conservative," so I ambled over to the student bookstore and bought a copy.

What I found was an imminently easy read of 150 pages. It was ghost-written yet surprisingly personal and talked about how to reclaim the American Dream through conservatism. Suddenly a light went on in my brain. I wanted more! The book struck a nerve albeit one that had been twitching just below the surface for a long time.

How Republicans can win in a changing America

I knew I needed to get involved, engaged and become more insightful - more consequential about what was going on around me. For the first time, I suspected that I, too, had an ideology and wanted to learn how to get other people to embrace it through political action. The question was, "How?"

After graduation, I decided to go to law school. All the while that unanswered question kept burning a hole in my brain, "Could the law be a way for me to accomplish my twin goals of having a respectable career that paid well <u>and</u> gave me an outlet for my interest in government and political theory?" After a year of burying my nose in law books, the answer for me was "no," especially after I heard a rousing talk given by the head of the Republican Party of Texas. It also seemed that passages from Goldwater's book were like signposts, directing me towards politics.

It was 1964. Along with four other law school students, I showed up on the doorstep of the Texas State Republican Party Headquarters and volunteered to help. We worked a few hours a week as the Party didn't have a formal staff. We helped them write their party platform, borrowing heavily from the GOP's California platform.

Later, in June, the Texas Republican Headquarters asked me to come to work for them full-time because Barry Goldwater had just gotten the nomination the previous day in California. Goldwater was off to a flying start having beaten Nelson Rockefeller in that primary. I was excited and shelved law school and worked my tail off all through the Fall on the campaign.

Imagine my surprise as a twenty-three year old young man when the Texas party head asked me to be Director of Research for the AU_4H_2O (Goldwater) for President Committee.

How Republicans can win in a changing America

My pride was ratcheted up even more when I saw my name on their organizational chart. Then reality set in. I had no idea what they expected of me. It didn't take long before I started reading the Congressional Quarterly and began dealing with the national press when they came through Texas.

My first campaign experience helped me shift gears and I started preparing reports on all sorts of issues like import beef quotas (this WAS Texas after all) even interpreting what they meant. All of a sudden, we get trounced two to one by Lyndon Johnson's camp. The experience taught me a lot and helped me establish a very important network which I would use very often, later on in life.

After your first campaign you have two choices: to throw in the towel or toughen up and come back stronger, later. I chose the latter.

The campaign was over and I was faced with a choice of what to do. After giving it a lot of thought, I decided I wanted to teach political science or government. The law would have to get along without Lance Tarrance as fate intervened. Before I could get into graduate school, Senator John Tower and Peter O'Donnell asked me to work full-time for the Republican Party and I was appointed the very first Director of Research for the Texas State Republican Party. I was now a full-time 'warrior' with more battles to prepare for.

One of my first jobs was to calculate the voters and voting histories of all of the 254 Texas counties on an old Underwood Olivetti machine (thank God it was electric). They needed to target all the places where they would need to get votes for GOP candidates. They told me it was going to take me a year.

I didn't relish the thought of a calculator as my new best friend, but I made the best of it. The takeaway of that experience for me was that research taught me that "I am not a tree guy, but a forest guy."

I realized that I didn't want to spend my life attached at the hip to a calculator, so in 1965 I found a guy who was starting up a computing company and posed this question to him, "What if we (the Republican Party) gave you all the publicity you could use in exchange for computerizing all our research?

Sure enough, he agreed and soon I was handing out reports left and right to all sorts of committee people who needed more in-depth knowledge about their own districts. This took me squarely into historical election research. Now THIS was getting interesting.

This brings me to the third stage of my education: public opinion and sample surveys. I'm now involved heavily in the 1966 John Tower re-election campaign. Like John Tower himself, the election was bombastic. It was a 'do or die' election. Either Tower wins and the Republican Party survives or he loses and the Party folds its tent. It was supposed to be a huge Republican defeat, but we won! During the election, I was asked to look at a lot of John Kraft's polls (Kraft was a pollster out of Chicago). Nobody really knew a lot about polling then, and I would be handed a poll and asked, "Do you understand what Kraft is telling us to do?"

Within two years of that experience I'm now playing in the big leagues. Because of all that work with the computing of historical statistics and polling, etc., I was asked to leave Texas and come to work for the RNC in Washington, DC. Football images came immediately to mind.

At that point in my life I felt more like a defensive coach, trying to gather information and intelligence to feed the offense a winning plan. Looking back today, I see my work as pioneering, a contribution to the whole polling process evolution. I guess that would make me a pioneer, too, though I certainly didn't think of myself as one way back then.

From Underwood Olivetti to IBM 360

The RNC was a political Petri dish where everything was growing. The use of computers was probably the most significant new development. I started using computers to not only tell us what the historical trends were, but I also used them for information retrieval at the RNC where we documented everything that the opposition candidates said, publicly.

We put all that data into an automatic retrieval system so that, for example, when candidate Nixon was on the plane, he'd get a speech that Hubert Humphrey had just made. That speech would be telecopied to us and an Eastman Kodak system would not only give us the speech in question but all the microfilm hits on what Humphrey had said earlier in his career on the same subject, many times contradicting his own current statements.

It pulled them all out, and we sent the whole kit and caboodle back to the Nixon plane. Then the Nixon press people would work with the national press people to counter a statement Humphrey made. What we really ended up doing was shortening the timeline for actively responding to candidates in a way that nobody had ever done before.

In 1968, this method and process was invaluable to our so-called 'truth squad' whose goal it was to hit the Democrats hard on their 'misstatements.'

How Republicans can win in a changing America

The apple of reward doesn't fall far from the tree of success. I got a lot of personal notoriety for devising the system, and it really boosted the *street cred* of the RNC as well because the Nixon campaign people didn't really have a lot of confidence in the RNC's capabilities to turn around the opposition's statements. They were always saying the RNC was just a bunch of bureaucrats. I've come to believe that our efforts really helped to change that attitude.

So we win and the Democrats are out of office for the first time in eight years. Nixon takes over the RNC and decides to clear out everybody that Ray Bliss had hired over the years. It was reorganized from 24 divisions to four and guess what? They ask this now 28 year-old to be one of the four new division heads. I'm now Director of Research for the whole national party and am over the moon about it.

I attribute a fair amount of my success to our ability to get accurate and timely data into the hands of decision-makers and do it systematically and consistently. At this point, I'm not a strategist; I'm an empiricist. The Nixon people decided to keep me at the RNC until just prior to the start of the 1970 Census. I was then asked to be Special Assistant to the Director of the Census (after a special civil service position was created).

The White House staff said, "If you see anything out there, numbers-wise, that could help us get re-elected, we want to know about it."

Those were pretty unambiguous marching orders and I took them to heart. I've got this great office out in Maryland, working with all the bureau chiefs and I'm looking over all the data that's coming in from the new U.S. Census and asking myself which of it might help us.

How Republicans can win in a changing America

I was a good marketing manager at the first stage of my career, but with my new Census experience I was getting more hands-on involvement in data collection and analysis. My education about public opinion research shifted into high gear.

I've often been asked, "Does a man need to be a good analyst to be a good strategist." The short answer is 'yes,' but it takes exposure to consistent and good data before any serious analysis can even begin. Without good data, good data management and reliable data collection, you simply can't develop good strategies. Lucky for me I was exposed to the right data and was able to recognize its value.

I even got the Bureau to send me to the University of Michigan to their Survey Research Center for about eight weeks. I poured over a mountain of data and was soon asked to write a book about 'ticket-splitting' which I later did.

What is ticket-splitting all about?

It became abundantly clear to me that if I wanted to make my mark on the political scene, I needed to get involved in polling in a big way. Dr. Walter DeVries knocked on my door in DC after reading some of the graduate research papers I wrote on split-ticket voting and suggested that we collaborate on a book on that very subject as he, too, had been giving it a lot of thought.

After pooling our notes we came up with a formula, using some of the polling data we had obtained from the (George) Romney for President Campaign. Then we married my academic research with his data to complete the "The Ticket-Splitter" which was published in 1972, thus revealing a whole new voter group that had spread across the whole country.

58

Ticket-splitters in particular don't follow either political party or offer anyone their complete allegiance. In the 70s, they manifested themselves on issues like education and the environment (what we might call 'suburban issues') and stayed away from the classic right-left issues. We identified people who were *habitual* in their split voting, that is changing their votes between the political parties and candidates on a single ballot.

We developed a profile of them, and that profile revealed that the majority were typically in their forties, educated and not ideologically-driven. They liked to select their candidates based upon their experience and their stance on the issues and not necessarily their political affiliation. Once we realized that this group was fairly substantial in size (about 20% of the total electorate) we came up with a formula that I later used in all my work to achieve a MWC (Minimum Winning Coalition). Here it is:

$$.90R + .65 \text{ T-S} + .30 \text{ WCD} = 51\% \text{ MWC}$$

(R = Republican, T-S = Ticket-splitter, WCD = White Conservative Democrats, MWC = Minimum Winning Coalition)

In order to win, we needed 90% of the Republican base vote which were straight party line voters or 'mostly' Republican voters. We called that our *base group*. Then we put together people who said they would vote for a few more Republicans than Democrats (or the reverse) as a behavioral measure. We called those the *swing/split group*. That was the group we needed to know more about because they could make or break us in future elections. We determined that we needed about 2/3 of this vote, plus the 90% of the Republican base to be competitive in any election. To find out more about them, we asked them another series of detailed questions. We asked about their ideology and of course their gender and race.

Not surprisingly, we found out that White Conservative Democrats (WCDs) and Moderate-to-Liberal White Democrats (MLWDs) were very high-potential areas for us, depending of course on the issues and the type of election. We determined that we needed roughly 30% of the WCDs in nearly any Congressional district or 10-15% of the MLWDs in order to push the election over 50% for us.

The African-American population was already voting 90% or more for the Democrats, so they were not a part of the formula (not because we didn't want them to come over to our side, but because the presumptive success probability was too low). Our formula was based on the <u>possible</u>, *not* on hope. We needed base Republicans, ticket-splitters and crossover issues voters.

In order to get to a realistic set of probabilities we had to resign ourselves to the fact that we were not going to get certain types of Democrats on our side, owing to the issues of the day. That was our normal formula, a formula for a minimum winning coalition. Then we would re-weight the data and try to find out how much more we had to squeeze out of these groups in order to win.

With all those possible voter combinations and coalitions we were able to develop not one campaign but about five mini-campaigns as we tracked support from Republicans through ticket-splitters and the other groups.

It worked so well in practice that we used it on every single survey we did, often monitoring the results throughout the entire two years or so of the election cycle. That way we were in 'real time' <u>all the time</u> with our data and knew exactly, sometimes as much as a month or two before the election, whether we had a chance to develop a minimum winning coalition. So from the time of our ticket-splitting model's use in

How Republicans can win in a changing America

the mid-70s, it became our 'calling card' and the brand mostly closely associated with my polling firm. The model became a key component of my selling proposition, and it's what separated me from all the other pollsters at the time.

No one else was actually putting the data into a formula that could be used throughout the election year to monitor the progress of the campaign AND be sensitive to changes in vote intentions. The model also gave us a chance to look at the complex multi-dimensional world of the American voter and not simply focus on a candidate's strengths and weaknesses. Ours was a value-added SWOT analysis. It was a formulistic, professional measurement and above all, successful.

In every survey we did, after the first cut of the data, we would run a new variable - a combined variable - of the following: voting behavior in past elections, ideology and race/gender. Those three questions were then re-combined into a single variable that would tell us how Republicans, ticket-splitters, WCDs and MLWDs (this included African Americans too) were thinking and reacting to questions posed in the survey.

In other words, it was the first prism we looked through for insight into their thought patterns. That breakout of the data gave us a pretty good idea of where the variances were so that we could clearly identify the likely sub-group voting patterns. The first thing we did was run this re-combined variable against every question on the survey. The results allowed us to write the best most correct strategy for the client's campaign, proving the value of the ticket-splitter model.

Polling software

Software packages were being just developed to help manage polling and I was interested in learning more, that was until a

How Republicans can win in a changing America

well-respected academic and big Nixon supporter by the name of Dr. David Derge came to me and said, "Don't worry about that, Lance. You can buy those things off-the-shelf. You need to learn how to interpret data. That's your key."

I took his advice and committed to get into public polling research, and with the momentum I got from my ticket-splitting book that had just come out (with favorable reviews by the Washington press corps), I was on my way. It was then I was asked to go to Harvard for a year to further my research, and that gave me time to put everything into perspective so that when I left Harvard I was ready to make my mark in the commercial world of polling.

Public, private and commercial polling

I ended my academic career with a Masters degree in political science and voting behavior, fields that gave me a sound foundation in the commercial world of polling, but I needed a paying job, tout de suite. I had to put that experience to work. But where? There was Lou Harris and Gallup but they were public pollsters and the universe of private polling was very small indeed.

After spending nearly seven years in DC, I managed to get a position with one of the new polling companies that were sprouting up. There were only two such firms: Market Opinion out of Detroit and DMI that was doing Reagan's governor work out of California.

(These were Republican firms doing Republican research and polling for the Republican Party, but they were something very new in the world of private polling.)

I opted for California and DMI and spent three good years there, adding to my knowledge about the business side of polling. After that, I was ready to set up my own company.

Polling to decision-making to the media

Good strategic decisions are not made in an information vacuum. They come from exhaustive analyses of survey data. I moved away from data and issue management into the rarefied atmosphere of public opinion polling to discover what voters were thinking. That not only put me in the campaign, it took me right up to the candidates themselves.

At DMI, I was not only asked to present data, but also to interpret it and tell them what it meant, which ultimately led to decisions on which TV spots or messages would hit their targets and 'sell' our candidates. At the tender age of 32, I'm now giving strategic advice to a variety of candidates on how to conduct their campaigns. Pretty heady stuff. I got the chance to express my world view and vision. Instead of reciting a bunch of numbers for the candidates, I decided to package them into a narrative form.

I wrote analyses, sometimes very long ones of 20 or 30 pages on how a situation, viewpoint or issue would play into the campaigns. Soon after, there were knocks on my door from a lot of folks asking me if this spot is right or if that tone is right. Is this a correct strategy? The other campaign heads knew they had to listen to us not only because we were good at our jobs and gave them a quality product, but also because they were afraid of getting too far off base...and being fired!

In short, everybody was hugging the numbers.

63

I soon discovered, after many long discussions with various campaign team members over a period of days and walking them through different scenarios, that the best way for our campaign to proceed was to let these people come to their own conclusions and not take them as gospel, directly from me.

I must have struck a nerve, because it worked. I quickly realized that it was my job to make the campaign manager look good, and it was possible through this simple but effective method of discussion, debate and decision. There is, however, an inherent danger in being too essential. Pollsters can delude themselves into believing they're more important than they really are - sometimes even more important than the candidates themselves. I managed to stay grounded and kept my distance from that trap.

I also kept my distance from the financial people - campaign donors. Believe me, there are many donors who want to snuggle up real close to the campaigns. Their presence can be disruptive to the campaigns, and the smell of their money can distract people from their jobs.

I'm 100% sure that donors in some campaigns, and on both sides of the aisle, have made bets with each other to see who was going to come out on top. I wanted no part of it at all. If they were going to make their beds they would have to lie in them...and lie in them alone without me. After all, there's no second place trophy in politics.

We maintained a kind of firewall, insulated ourselves, so that we could concentrate on working with the media consultants, the candidates and their campaign managers and other select personnel. These were usually very productive relationships based on trust and a strong value proposition.

How Republicans can win in a changing America

I've often been asked how a Republican pollster can work with Republican candidates and remain unbiased. I liken it to the Cold War. If you worked both sides of THAT street, sooner or later one of your employers would liquidate you.

You had to be objective and truthful while serving only one master. Many of our campaigns had an overarching goal, and that was to win a solid majority of the vote that would enable us to really influence the body politic of the U.S. That meant that everybody HAD to work together even if it wasn't directly.

I also worked closely with the media consultants who were generally the first to be hired. I realized early on that they wanted the political strategist/polling experts to help them develop some of their messages. The media consultants pushed me and wanted me to analyze verbatim responses not just summary statistics. That meant that I needed to once again write more in-depth analyses and distribute them widely.

Each consultant/strategist who received my analyses knew they had something of value. Their usual reply was, "That's really different. Most pollsters don't do that. They just leave us with numbers and no real interpretation or analysis."

The more value and information my clients got the more they wanted it operationalized in much the same way as I had done for Nixon back in '72. I replayed in my mind all the football games I'd seen in my life and tried to make strategic and organizational connections with politics.

That led me to developing my 'Four Corners Offense,' a formula of how to conduct winning campaigns. I was moving from being a mere defensive coach to more of an offensive coach that must smell victory.

65

It was a stakeholder approach that included how to address communication needs and how to form campaign coalitions to win. Pretty soon it started to make sense (thankfully) to those who were exposed to it.

The Four Corners Offense (FCO)

As in sports, the political field is a proving ground, or battlefield, where we test our strengths and strategies.

In the early 80s, I was moving quickly up the ladder towards the next rung of strategic analysis from interpreting demographic and voting behavior. During that time I realized, that like in football, there was a 'hole in our line' (the entire campaign process) that nobody in the polling field was moving in to fill.

Basically, that *hole* was the absence of a coherent strategy to alternately defend and attack at will - and anticipate the opposition's moves. For example, after a survey was done, it was delivered to the candidate where it was then dissected and presented during a typical 2-3 hour session - mostly summarizing mere aggregate numbers. Unfortunately, after all that work, many campaigns reverted to some of their old bad habits.

They just didn't see the value in interpreting beyond the numbers. They were also not disciplined enough to stay on message, making things worse, kind of like a patient who gets good prescriptive advice from his doctor and then ignores it. This was frustrating for all of us, so I vowed to correct the problem. As I have done so many times before, my thoughts went to the strategic side of sports. I immersed myself in the whole campaign process and then into each aspect of it to clearly see its relationship to the others.

I started with campaign communications. The media consultants at that time would usually come up with media spots, often based on their own intuition, <u>even after reading the polling data that could be pointing them in a different direction.</u> While many of them were getting awards for creativity they weren't necessarily winning campaigns with them.

It was obvious to me that we needed to link our campaign messages with our polling results, so we did just that and developed our communications strategy based on our polling data. We looked beyond our own biases of the present, off into the future where the numbers were telling us we needed to be.

The subconscious is an exciting place. Unfortunately, we can't usually visit it while we're in a conscious state.

Every so often, human beings have flashes that cut through the barrier separating the two. One of mine, the Four Corners Offense, was an epiphany borrowed from the offense of the same name created by the famous basketball coach Dean Smith from the University of North Carolina at Chapel Hill. Smith's strategy was actually developed to 'run out the clock' when his team was ahead. Mine was different, though it did have some similarities with the great coach's.

Visualize a basketball court. Now visualize the players. There's a center, two guards and two forwards. In my FCO, the center represents the candidate. The two forwards and guards (communications, polling/data-gathering, analysis and strategizing) produced the points. Before anyone could suit up or take to the *court*, I decided that I needed to simplify the whole campaign structure and learn how to concentrate and focus our methods on our objectives.

I remembered, that in the military, an officer is taught to find the weaknesses in the enemy's lines using good intel so that when his unit fires into that zone they will literally break the enemy in two. My *fire zone* was the <u>messaging</u> of the campaign, an area of critical importance that would break down the Democrat opponent while we stayed on message and kept pouring it on until we split their ranks. THAT was the idea of the Four Corners Offense, and to be successful with it, you had to be disciplined and know your issues and voter groups inside and out and keep the pressure on the opponent.

The FCO had to be based on the best data possible and a thorough knowledge of your opponent. That means that no messaging should be done without a touch-back to the research. *(Though I call it an 'offensive' strategy, it is very much a defensive one, too, the defensive part being rooted in opposition research and in the responses from our survey questioning.)*

To make any strategy work, you must first have information, purposeful debate, communication, cohesion, a clear, workable plan and discipline. The final component is vision. Each member of the team is a two-way conduit for plays coming from the bench through the team captain and then back from the players who reported on the opponents' weaknesses or tactics.

Here's an example of how the whole thing works: For a Republican client I would usually take a tax or government management issue that we got from our survey, one where we knew the Democrats were vulnerable. We would make that one of our four corners. Then we would do up, in virtual reality, TV spots, speeches and direct mail on that particular issue.

Every time we mentioned that issue we knew we were going to go up against one of the Democrats' major long-term issues as well which might be more government services, for example.

How Republicans can win in a changing America

The two would be in active competition with each other. I would do the same thing for the Democratic opposition candidate based on what we knew about him and the Democrats' strategies and messages along with which issues they planned on dominating. In other words, we matched up an FCO against the Democrats' attack themes.

The idea was to match up your best player with your opponent's - or you found the opposition's weakness so you could exploit it and win more points. Each of these issues would be used to accelerate dominance by the Republican candidates, pitting them against the Democrats (and their issue stances) so that you had a clear and predictable field. It was a calculated play, designed to run through scenarios in virtual reality before we went to the expense of doing our TV buys, spots and message development for real.

We'd do it for all sorts of issues like education, border security, job growth, to name three more. Internally, we had to agree on the top four issues that would net us points (votes) and then do our due diligence on them. It was critical that we all were on the same page and that no resources or attention were diverted away from these issues. Focus, focus, focus.

We knew that once the gloves were off and our opponents saw our spots they'd counter, hard. Our task was to be ready (we had already run through the likely scenarios and had anticipated their moves and had counter-messages in place). This was the quickest and most likely road to success. As in basketball, we needed to hold their point tally down by using a one-on-one and occasionally all-on-one offense. Knowing that one of their players (think of a player as an issue) averaged 25 points a game, we knew that we wouldn't be able to hold him to zero, but maybe 10-12 points was possible.

69

THAT would be net eight points in our favor, and this point/issue advantage would be factored into our pre-arranged formula for achieving a minimum winning coalition in that particular campaign.

Our success was always dependent upon focus, discipline and teamwork. Each part of the campaign had to be in synch with the others. All rallied around the meta-message or the central message of the campaign that evolved from the surveys and eventually formed not only the campaign strategy but also influenced the candidate profile.

Every time an issue came up that didn't fit into this profile or this FCO we would deal with it without taking our eye off the ball (the four main issues). We were not going to be goaded into making immediate off-the-cuff statements or worse yet, be pulled into what we called, 'cul-de-sacs' in which we would end up in a perpetual circle of confusion perpetrated by our opponents.

Campaigns can be confusing, but campaign/candidate messages should NEVER be confusing. We avoided confusion by graphing out the messages, counter-messages and counter-counter messages that would be employed by our opponents and did the same in reverse.

We transferred them to overlays and laid them on top of one another so that all campaign team members could see the whole picture (it was like playing three dimensional chess where you saw many moves in many different combinations ahead of you). We pounded the internal message, the so-called meta-message or over-arching message (or theme if you will) that was set up by the Four Corners message we had chosen, because we knew that THAT was the deciding message - the one voters (especially ticket-splitters) - would hone in on with their votes.

70

The FCO had far-reaching benefits. It forced everybody out of their individual silos or stovepipes and showed them the value of a team approach and an orchestrated coherent message. I was asked by more than one campaign manager about one issue or another, and since we had already spent two days developing our strategy I would say, "Tell me where in our strategy that fits?"

Sometimes they'd say that it didn't fit and I'd say, "Then forget it unless you want to do another survey and adjust your entire campaign." If they said, yes, and wanted another survey, it was an indication that the campaign wasn't doing well. When I walked away from a campaign where the FCO was employed, I always knew that we had done our best because we had focused on the facts that came to us via the survey data and then extrapolated them to a campaign plan.

Any other post-mortem investigation would have to concentrate on the human element and the decisions that were made with that data. I still use the Four Corners Offense in my daily life. I think Dean Smith would be proud to see his strategy for running out the clock morph into one that used time wisely right from the start of the game AND got points on the board with the best matchup strategy.

I had three years with DMI and then ten good years on my own where I operationalized all those hundreds of thousands of pages of data and turned them into winning strategies. Whenever we employed the Four Corners Offense and tested it in real life, it worked because each campaign had a stake in the outcome.

Maybe I went from coaching to architect, because I've been able to take a clear vision or design and turn it into a successful structure by understanding the principals of sound building techniques AND because I was able to speak the language of the construction bosses to motivate them to implement that vision without risking the integrity of the building.

Prescriptions and personalities: Polling is really hard work

I can remember a Louisiana Congressman once told me, "Lance, of all the consultants I've ever talked to, you're the only one that has the data AND can see the end of the game before it's played." Very flattering, indeed, but he was on to something.

Political polling is really a science, but there may be some artistry involved. Sadly, many pollsters today are not statistically trained as they should be. The reasons are those nifty software packages that will do all the statistical work for you. The bottom line is that pollsters now are more political than statistical. The generation I evolved from was very strong on demographics. And statistical routines? We knew how they worked.

These days it's kind of an erector set exercise. Hopefully, the new pollsters will learn how critical basic data-gathering, statistical analysis and demographic knowledge are to their success and to the success of their candidates. While polling is a science, it merges nicely with the art of strategizing. If I had jumped into strategy too early, I wouldn't have grown the 'wisdom teeth' I needed to chew through the numbers and give me the experience and confidence to make suggestions to many a campaign manager and candidate.

I believe that truly successful quarterbacks are born that way. You need certain gifts that you cannot learn but which can be cultivated and enhanced through intense practice and focused study.

Jack Kemp once said to me that when he was tackled right after throwing a long pass, he *saw* the pass as being completed even while he lay near unconscious at the bottom of hundreds of pounds of the opposing team's players. He <u>knew</u> it was going to connect. That's the mark of an inspired or perhaps *born* quarterback.

The art of the science is taking what you know factually, combining it with instinct, intuition and knowledge of human behavior and then coming up with a few possible courses of action or options. I've always been a conservative populist in terms of my preferences for campaign styles and I was even referred to by Ronald Brownstein as the only conservative populist pollster in the Republican Party.

He also said something nice about me that I really appreciated, that I was one of only a few pollsters who had the vision to see the whole game - from start to finish before it was played. There is a danger though. You must not see yourself as infallible and start believing your own PR. You cannot push yourself past the data or brush it aside before you've given it enough time to make sense to you. There is a distinct pathway you must travel with data in hand and it is the universally accepted method of the scientist.

If your client is below 50% on the ballot question, irrespective of his lead, you're not ready to win. Hypothesize the reasons, but don't restrict yourself to the paths that will only reinforce your hypothesis. While you should not subordinate your vision to your data, you should not let your vision manage the outcomes, either. You must keep both in balance and at the forefront of your mind at all times. Many people have had grand visions for the Republican Party, and I had mine, too. I was tired of seeing 21% voter (party) identification for the Republicans. I knew we wouldn't get to 50% unless we did something different.

73

I came from a state that had a pitiful 14% Republican identification. Today, we hold every single position and every statewide office in Texas. But the bottom line is you don't win that kind of support by appealing solely to Republican voters, and that's why I went more populist and encouraged my clients to do the same.

We needed to appeal to the downscale, middle-class voter as well. I started pushing this conservative populism and fellows like the late Lee Atwater did too. I remember many private sessions together where Lee and I traded books back and forth and vowed to get Reagan into a more populist communication mode.

That's what we used to call, "common sense - uncommon courage," something Texan Phil Gramm used in his own campaign. It's nothing mystical or magical. It simply means having the courage to say things like they should be said and then packaging them together with a common sense message of why we feel the way we do. On the subject of truthfulness, a pollster or strategist MUST tell his candidate the truth <u>every single step of the way</u> or he's a liability to the campaign.

Here's a little story about that very thing...

Al Fay was a national committeeman and wanted to run for Governor in the State of Texas. He commissioned me to do a survey for him, and that survey was done of Republican voters. Well, sure enough, it came back and the result was, and I had to tell him this, "They know who you are, but they don't think you should run." He said, "Lance, I've got all the money in the world. I need to run." *(Fay even told the press at one point that, "I am a one-man conglomerate" after having revealed his vast financial holdings in 23 businesses).*

How Republicans can win in a changing America

I said, "That doesn't matter. You're not going to get elected." Admittedly, there are times when you don't *want* to tell your candidates the truth. One example is when the candidate is so far ahead in the polls, and you've told him he's got the wind at his back. The fear is he might slow down and become complacent.

I don't like negative campaigning and don't get involved in it, but I would hear things. For example, Tom Bradley, son of sharecroppers and grandson of slaves and successful mayor of Los Angeles and odds-on favorite to be the next governor of California had a Horatio Alger image. He was born in Texas, was a track star, police chief, mayor. He seemed unbeatable.

But WE beat him, and one of the ways we beat him was by doing research on everything he'd done. We found out that in Santa Monica Bay they had been cited twice by the Feds for dumping sewage in the bay. Well, each time, the city government (and he was the mayor) never did anything about it. We knew that environmental initiatives were going to be on the ballot that year, and it appeared to be the perfect opportunity to use that example of his decision-making (or lack thereof) as a reason not to vote for him.

We managed to suck him into a debate early on. We talked about how Republican Governor George Duekmejian had cleaned up several toxic waste sites during his administration. This affected the Bradley campaign tremendously, so much so that they went out and borrowed a lot of money and tried to go toe-to-toe with us on the record. But it didn't work.

Opposition research is not a noble endeavor, but it's necessary. The public knows it. The media knows it and the candidates know it. Everybody knows it.

How Republicans can win in a changing America

We can decry it. We can describe it as despicable and degrading to the political process, but the facts don't change its necessity.

Opposition research in and of itself is kind of worthless unless you do something with it. I believe that if you have evidence that pinpoints the mistakes the other candidate has made and you're going use it, you had better point to something positive your candidate has done to make the contrast with your candidate a stark one. The strategy should never be, 'fight on somebody else's battlefield.'

Getting your message out to the right people

There are a number of reputable public polling companies, among them Gallup and the Pew Research Center that are leading the pack. There are about twelve companies offering national polls. Now some of them are Democrat firms that say they're non-partisan, but they really aren't.

Then you have the private polling companies, and typically they don't release data, though private pollsters may release data on certain occasions when they feel it's critical that their client get that little bit of informational boost by sending their polls to the press. The press actually wears two hats: one of so-called independent journalists and one of pollsters. Many have their own polling organizations, and they would obviously rather rely on their own polling results than those of other companies that might have an agenda different from their own.

The typical telephone poll is 1,000 interviews taking 18 minutes. In one-third of those we want to know the exact demographics of the interviewees. The second third we'd poll on was for the long-term factors on what the interviewees felt about what was going on in the current administration on issues like, "was economics trumping defense," etc.

We use this to get a handle on the subjects' long-term values. The final third was just *fishing*, looking for the small nuances - the untold stories, things that might break open a race.

<u>Social media has made polling much more difficult.</u>

In the old days, polling was done through personal household interviews where, on a statewide basis, you might need to hire 10-12 local research companies to do the job. Primary sampling units (PSUs) describe these personal interviews that were basically done door-to-door.

Gallup and Harris did them, and they would end with a questionnaire that would be filled out and sent back. That's why Gallup was wrong in 1948 when they predicted a win for Thomas Dewey. <u>They didn't get the information back from these household interviews until early October and they failed to update any further change in the electorate!</u>

Door-to-door household polling really didn't cut it. Further exacerbating the difficulties were the riots of '68. Companies simply said it was too dangerous to go house-to-house and decided to do telephone polling, instead. It was a lot easier to do random polling. Using a fixed list is very tight and has better confidence intervals. It's simply better, statistically.

Back then, 90% of households had a fixed-line telephone as contrasted with the recent boom in mobile phone use. Polls today are becoming less accurate not more accurate. This is not because the science is bad. It's because the marketplace is changing so fast. We have seen a predictable progression from in-home polling to telephone polling and now to mobile phone polling, made necessary because so many households have dropped their fixed lines. That includes the Internet and other ways people are getting their information.

How Republicans can win in a changing America

A typical interview today is half fixed-lines and half mobile. This has led to some companies switching to Internet polling for specific voter segments.

Just think about the specific issues where polling is done by email. Let's take the Farm Bill that was debated this year. You have 5,000 farmers. Each has an email address and each can be sent an email and asked a question. Then those responses are sent back to the polling organization within minutes or a few hours. The impact can be crucial to a Congressional vote.

The future may well hold that Internet polling has become the most significant change in polling methodology. It could be that one day large numbers of respondents will answer with a click of a mouse. We're already doing it for sub-groups like the farmers. It's not statistically perfect yet because you must weight those respondents very carefully so that you're not just taking the opinions of people whose views you already know.

When Gallup predicted Dewey's win, they were actually right <u>at the time of their sampling.</u> Unfortunately, they stopped polling around October 10th. Now, of course, the company says it will never do THAT again. The same general principal was working in the election of 2012 except that we had an expectation level that may have been unreasonably high.

Polling to those expectations (even though they were grounded in the Census of 2010) and simply adjusting the weights was wrong. The turnout models were also all out of whack. What we should have looked at was a voter's ideological belief in either a welfare state or a limited government state.

<u>Almost nobody got it right.</u>

The Democrats claimed that they got it right so let's give them credit. They won. They had better statistics and better information and they carefully tracked their success with special sub-groups like women and labor unions. They said, "We're not going to accept a formula that worked eight years ago. We've created a new one." They were not accepting certain absolutes like they were going to get 93% of the Black vote, for example.

They wanted to get a higher <u>overall turnout</u> like 13% instead of just 10%. That's huge! What they did was re-weight the basic American formula. Unfortunately for the Republicans, there was a significant drop in the turnout of registered White voters, to make matters worse.

<u>We should have gotten *our* voters out to vote.</u>

We don't know why they stayed home. Was it because Romney was perceived to be an elitist? Did he ignore the Tea Party and the growing populism from the 2010 election? Between the low White voter turnout which did blow the polls and the extra points from the *welfare state* groups that were hyped-up, all the 'normal vote' numbers were thrown out. Let's not blame the pollsters too much.

As I said earlier, the science is sound. Gallup's registered voter turnout model worked. They had Obama ahead by one point. While we believed there would be a slight drop in the turnout of registered voters, we still thought that Obama would lose by two points. It's the likely voter model that got pollsters in trouble because they assigned these coefficients to each one of those voter turnout groups. Let's face it. If you're getting a lot of money from the Federal Government, then the last thing you want is a limited or downsized Federal Government.

If you fear that your food stamps will be taken away or that you'll get no health care program, then you're <u>not</u> going to vote for the candidates who are for smaller leaner government. It seems like we've gone from voting our national interests to protecting our own self-interests in one fell swoop.

That has thrown off the polling, big time. There's a struggle going on among academics about this new wave of Internet polling and the principal area of concern is its lack of accuracy. This takes me back to the 1936 election when Alf Landon was running. His campaign at the time felt that they had a pretty substantial advantage because they only looked at the polling information that was sent back from people they knew very well.

Actually, Landon was predicted to win by the Literary Digest as that company had only looked at their own subscribers' responses to a survey. Pollsters today are justifiably worried because they don't want to overcompensate for the new social media. The different sampling frame they're now using with 50% mobile phones is also of concern to them.

Pew and the Wall Street Journal/NBC polls are probably the two best polls right now reaching out with new technology. Those using social media, exclusively, probably have the least likelihood of turning out to vote. Pollsters must add this in as a possible 'flag' to look at. Polls must be more personality-oriented than issues-oriented when it comes to doing turnout predictions, but the pollsters should also be concerned that they don't get out too far ahead of the social media area lest they repeat the election of 1936.

One of the companies that has moved exclusively into Internet sampling is the Economist in London which has a good following here in the U.S. among business elites.

How Republicans can win in a changing America

The Economist and YouGov are two organizations that have joined forces. You'll often see them referred to as the Economist/YouGov.

What they're attempting to do is weight their data because their interviewees are on the Internet, exclusively. Most respondents are paid to answer the questions. So, if you want a quick poll done, you can go to them (because it's a very homogeneous group) and you can take that to Congress and tell them that you've just done a 500-person poll and 'X' is the result. These polls are pretty powerful and they will influence legislators.

I see these Internet polls not specifically used for Presidential races. They will be done more for lobbying and issue development. Issue development is a very different polling procedure than for candidate polling. It's more a niche polling technique for issue development.

Significant differences exist between random samples and the type of polling done by the Economist/YouGov. For example, their recent poll showed the President's approval rating down fifteen points where random sampling only showed five.

The other development in polling is TV network polling. Today, a poll cannot be put out for purely propaganda purposes without it being countered by the media (network) polls. In public polling, if you're off by too much, you'll lose your credibility and the networks won't even pick up your polls. There's a very short half-life for pollsters who are too bombastic and too incestuous with their polls.

(Some of the smaller pollsters that have worked for Congressional candidates have also had trouble getting traction and credibility for their candidates because they're up against a long-term incumbent.)

How Republicans can win in a changing America

We believe, that in the U.S., we can re-weight data almost ad infinitum to get us closer to the realistic situation such as knowing the differences in the various sub-group electorate numbers. Some of the changes in society such as the increased incidence of multiple generations living in the same home can be handled through the effective use of screening questions, for example.

If we know for a fact that the statistics will prove that there is a substantial difference in a sampling, we will simply re-weight the poll instead of interviewing more subjects. This a common practice among all pollsters. The challenge for the Internet pollsters is to try to re-weight their very rarefied samples and make them more traditional.

They're going to have to do a lot of statistical weighting to achieve what the Census Department says is the accurate profile of the American demographic. The Gallup Registered Voter model turned out to be a correct one.

Our country is turning towards more government intervention, more government group thinking and government management of outcomes. Many in the lower economic classes that would vote 30% of the time are now voting 60% of the time though they're nowhere near the 85-90% of the white-collar suburban educated voters. That's where we went wrong in the 2012 election. Obama was able, through welfare recipients, through government, to access the welfare class to make promises that were way beyond his or government's ability to keep.

The Obama people have defied some of the historical norms. They were able to re-engineer the universe to bring in younger voters, welfare-positive voters and young women beyond their normal (historical) turnout.

How Republicans can win in a changing America

There is a demographic bulge coming, too, and it is the Hispanic vote. Only 1% of the total voter turnout in the election of 1980 was Hispanic. Now it's 10%. That's a pretty big jump from one generation to the next.

The Hispanic vote will be big next time because technically they are larger than the African-American population. These statistics were based on the exit polls from the last election. There was a slight uptick in 2008 with young people who thought that Obama was a transformational figure - a white knight riding in to save America. During the Vietnam War years, a lot of reporters said that the youth vote was going to change America. Politicians were worried about the 18-24 year olds coming onto the voter rolls and up-ending the status quo, but that wave was offset by blue-collar workers. What the media forgot were all those young conservative people in the labor force.

The 1970 census was unique because this was the first time we allowed people to self-indicate their ethnicity (Hispanic for example) as well as their race. I'm sure this didn't make Black America happy as it effectively bumped them lower on the Census' top minority race/ethnicity scale.

Between the elections of 2008 and 2012, the youth vote effectively lost half its power. I believe that this indicates that the youth vote was an episodic situation as it was based upon the White Knight theory (I'll explain that later).

This group should be pretty depressed and disgusted with the Obama Administration right now given the decisions that have actually marginalized them or relegated them to the unemployment rolls...or their parents' basement. If their expectations continue to be unmet and the Administration's promises remain un-kept, we may see this voter group stay home in future elections.

83

The other impending bulge is the 'baby boomers' who are entering the Social Security rolls at the rate of 10,000/day. These people are not, generally speaking, of the same political stripe as those 18-24 year olds. That's why we need to watch and track them.

Real people, real campaigns

In 1978, John Tower was running for a Senate seat from Texas, and at a point he was way behind the eight-ball. He had a pretty messy divorce. He had backed Ford against Reagan which was a bad move, and he couldn't even get a seat at the convention.

Add to that he was considered to be the easiest Senator to be defeated in the 1978 election and it was apparent we had a steep uphill climb ahead of us. He was running up against a Democrat Congressman by the name of Bob Krueger who had a PhD in English Literature (not exactly the mold of a typical Texas Senator). We were losing and the Democrats were putting up polls saying that Tower was going down.

We found, through opposition research, that Krueger had voted twice to give the District of Columbia two Senators. We discovered in our polling that this was definitely an issue that Texas Republicans wanted no part of.

We also found out that Democrats bristled at the notion, so we used that polling and the media people created a TV spot that said that Bob Krueger actually wanted two Senators named in the District of Columbia which would effectively cancel out our two-Senator vote in Texas. *(That included Democratic Senator Lloyd Bentsen, so that really put Democrats on the fence!)* There was cross pressure going into the election, and it was one of the things that turned the election around AND it came straight out of the polling, polling I was doing for Tower at the time.

How Republicans can win in a changing America

As a former science professor, Tower was very appreciative and understanding of polling and was aware of its importance to his campaign.

I attribute part of his success to that attitude. There was no delay in going from important polling data right to the media. I remember, along with thousands of other Texans, the famous *non-handshake incident* when Krueger, who was running nasty media ads disparaging Tower's family, walked over to Tower after a political event and stuck out his hand. Tower refused it. A photo was taken and sent to the wire services and soon our campaign was losing its steam among voters who had seen it and had now deemed the Senator to be unfriendly or an elitist.

The truth lay elsewhere.

The Senator was angry about the nasty ads Krueger was running. We soon hit the telephones and I taped a number of interviews and took them up to the Senator's HQ in Austin and played them for him. After listening intently, he soon realized that he had to do something and do something fast because he had been stonewalling up to that point.

The campaign recorded a spot for him where he was seated looking straight into the lens. The camera whirred, and he told Texans that, "For months my opponent has continued a campaign of unabated distortion and deception. I think he has engaged in scurrilous campaign activities which Texans do not admire. I think under the circumstances that I should not have dignified him by shaking his hand after what he's engaged in."

Tower went on to talk about his father who told him that when you shake a man's hand it is a gesture of friendship, trust and respect and that he had neither for Mr. Krueger.

How Republicans can win in a changing America

Tower also said that he believed people in Texas didn't want a man who talked out of both sides of his mouth. The *indignation spot* worked. Tower squeaked out a win with 0.3% more votes than Krueger.

The year is 1980 and Governor John Connally of Texas is getting ready to run for President. George H.W. Bush and others are also running, but many of the power brokers felt that Connally was the ideal candidate.

He was a Democrat turned Republican, was very decisive and had enormous personal charisma. We knew our road was going to be a rocky one because the Governor was not a 'real' Republican. That haunted us all the way through. Unfortunately, we had a bigger problem. It was Governor Connally's arrogance. He used to tell us that if he could talk to every voter one-on-one he'd win an election in a minute, so strong was his feeling about his own power of persuasion.

Five Presidential leadership styles

Years ago, we did a lot of research on Presidential leadership styles. We came up with five top ones. Once you get past voter ideology (which is extremely hard to change) the selection of a President becomes a very personal one that is based on leadership style. We identified five distinctly different styles from a number of focus groups and discussions with countless individuals.

The first style was the so-called *Great Manager*, a President with extraordinary management skills that would be brought to bear to the job. The second was the *Super Politician*, someone who could legislate and reach across the aisle to make deals and avoid gridlock.

The third was the *Caretaker*, a highly ethical, perhaps extremely religious man who would appeal to those wanting a moral role model.

The fourth was the *Problem-Solver*, a pragmatic President that would eschew ideology and instead focus on the politics of the possible. The fifth was the *White Knight*, an outsider who would come in, and through the sheer force of his personality and innovative ideas, change things for the better - clean house.

JFK was considered a White Knight even though we know that this was part of his carefully managed image. In many ways, Reagan was one too, an outsider, an actor. John Connally said he didn't need polls to lead him. He would lead the polls. He grew up in a generation where politickin' was done through personal contact and power.

While making my presentation on the five Presidential leadership types, Connally interrupted me and took issue with my characterization of him as a 'White Knight.' He felt that if that was somebody like Jack Kennedy, he didn't want to be in the same neighborhood with him let alone the same category. He had a long-standing memory of the LBJ/Bobby Kennedy enmity in his early years as a Democrat.

At that point, my presentation was over as far as the Governor was concerned, all because of the Kennedy bias. He didn't want that JFK shadow anywhere near him. To be honest, this stubbornness messed up our whole campaign. Connally went from the cover of Time magazine to getting only one delegate...from Arkansas. The last days of the campaign were truly miserable. He brought in a bunch of his friends, former Democrats, and it all spiraled downwards from there. His was one of the most ignominious defeats in all of American political primary history.

87

This only goes to prove that in politics, polling matters. And if you continue to ignore the results and only listen to your own inner voice, it may well be the only voice you hear at the end of the day because the truth-tellers will have deserted you.

The end of a chapter

I sold my company in 1990. The last real Presidential election I worked in was 1988. Twenty-four years in Presidential politics had taught me an awful lot. I was not involved in the 1992 election and wasn't there to see George H. W. Bush lose. I had learned from the Goldwater effort, from the Nixon wins in recovery and demise, from the Reagan insurgencies, from the Bush *41* late developing victory in '88. After all that, I was ready for a new challenge.

Then came McCain.

When John McCain was running for an open seat in the First Congressional District in Arizona in 1982, there were a dozen others running for the same seat. We were asked by McCain's consultant to do the polling. Actually, we did a survey on all the Republican candidates, and it turned out that John McCain was leading the entire pack and would have had the votes to get the nomination. (It was a winner-take-all situation and not a majority decision.)

I clearly remember calling McCain's people and saying that he should not get out of the race even though his people were ready to pull the plug and go! They wanted him to run in another election, later, when the field wasn't so crowded. I must have said it forcefully enough and with enough conviction because McCain stayed in the race.

How Republicans can win in a changing America

John remembered that survey and my plea. Eighteen years passed and I'm sitting on my porch overlooking the lake and I get a call. The voice at the other end says, "Hi, Lance. It's John McCain." I didn't believe it was him. I thought it was one of my practical joker buddies pulling my leg.

After a minute or two, I was finally convinced that it was McCain. (This is before the 2000 New Hampshire Primary and he was calling to see if I was committed to another candidate like Bush). I was flattered, but I was now back in 'Bush country' in Texas, so I decided that my best course of action was to wait it out.

In 2004, I indirectly helped out the George W. Bush team by going to Washington and worked with the U.S. Chamber of Commerce on an independent expenditure. It was my job to devise some strategy and policy that would basically oppose the candidacy of John Edwards, the Vice Presidential candidate selected by John Kerry. So you can say that I dipped my toe back into the political waters for about three months. I felt I needed a change of scenery so I was glad to be back in Washington.

In 2006, I got a call from John McCain's 'Straight Talk America' PAC. They asked me if I would join them. I became a Senior Strategist and gave them my vision of where McCain should use his energy in his future campaign. He was going to need a seasoned professional like myself who could look beyond the 24-hour news cycle and see the 4th quarter. They wanted (and desperately needed) long-term thinking and long-term planning.

After awhile, we transferred into real jobs on the campaign in January 2007. People around John McCain and many in the national press thought he would be the nominee and most likely face Hillary Clinton for the Presidency, and as a result didn't entertain too many contrary opinions.

89

McCain got in trouble with a lot of folks because of his aggressive stance on Iraq and his legislative work with Ted Kennedy on immigration reform. His trip back to DC during the economic meltdown puzzled a lot of people, too, and threw up a big question mark on his insight into the economy.

In the summer of 2007, the McCain campaign actually went bankrupt and folded. At that point, everybody was cut loose, including yours truly. I continued to work pro bono for McCain up through December of 2007. After he became the nominee by default, the RNC took over the campaign and actually ran it as an institutional campaign...a big mistake.

One very disappointing factor was that John didn't want to be bothered by polling. On the spectrum of true believers he was somewhere between John Connally and John Tower. Every polling exercise we had for McCain went to his staff, and I'm still not sure to this day how many polls he really read. Fortunately, his staff was pretty savvy about polling.

As far as leadership types go, I think that John would probably self-identify with the Super Politician, somebody who could work both sides of the aisle searching for support for compromise legislation. That was his style. He was not a White Knight, though the country seemed desperately poised for one.

There is another thing that I think John discovered from his 2008 run and that was the enormous difficulty associated with being a full-time Senator and a full-time Presidential candidate. It's just impossible to do unless of course you put your senate portfolio on the shelf like the current inhabitant of the White House did.

Polling and the money men

Polling is extremely crucial to find-raising. As I mentioned earlier, about 50% of the country will throw their weight behind a candidate that advocates their ideology. The other 50% simply want to play with a winner.

That second group is constantly being fed polling results from the campaign's managers. It's similar to Wall Street when a broker does his due diligence and research so that he can back up his stock recommendations when speaking to his clients. Throughout my entire career, I'm proud to say that I kept the firewall up between myself and the financial people. I felt it was ethically right and the professional thing to do.

The year 1980 was a real wild year. I was asked to go to Arkansas and do some polling for a Texas-born candidate by the name of Frank White. The goal was to knock Bill Clinton off his new left-leaning Governor's perch. The Clinton camp was an interesting one. Clinton had brought in a lot of former McGovern staffers from the time he headed up the McGovern volunteer effort in Texas. This new, young, left-of-center crowd, resplendent in their beards and ponytails, were his *brain trust*, his inner circle.

Unfortunately for him, this group was too loopy. His new political laboratory was backfiring on him. Then Clinton did something that I suspect he regrets even to this day. He decided to nearly double Arkansas's license plate fees which affected nearly every good ole boy driving a pickup truck. For many in that group that voted for the youngest governor in Arkansas's history, this was the last straw. The furor included drivers and voters from both parties. This was especially true of the working class male voter. It was a true blue- collar vs. elite situation.

91

And then a Democrat, who was nothing more than a proud and angry pickup truck owner who opposed Governor Clinton's policies, threw his hat in the ring. At the end of the day, at primary time, he ended up getting 37% of the Democrat vote!

We managed to persuade a fellow by the name of Frank White to run. Frank was a converted Republican but very much a concerted Democrat, so we decided to go after Democrat voters because polling showed us that if we only cultivated the Republican vote we would lose. So we played to that White conservative base of the Democrat Party.

I got a call at 10:00 am the morning after Election Day. Reagan had won and I was feeling pretty good, so I answered the phone cheerily. It was Frank White and he sounded a bit shocked. He said he'd won by 32,000 votes and then said almost as an aside, "They tell me I need to have a transition team. What's that?" This should have given me a clue as to how his administration would govern for the next two years.

Two years later, in 1982, the economy was in the dumps with 10% unemployment. That was just too much for Republicans in state elections. We lost thirteen governorships that year and Arkansas's was one of them. Bill Clinton did something interesting after his loss of the Governorship in 1980.

Shortly after the election, in February, he bought a large block of media time during which he told the Arkansas people that he was sorry he let them down ("I'm sorry I messed up."). In other words, it was a big mea culpa and a bold and successful move on Clinton's part. It worked to soften the voters' resistance to him for his next political run.

How Republicans can win in a changing America

The unmaking of a mistake

I'll end this chapter with the unmaking of a mistake. About four months after the election of Frank White, I was invited to come to the University of Arkansas to give a lecture. One of the interesting things I found in doing research for the lecture was a survey question about Hillary's resistance to change her name to that of her husband's.

So I mentioned this in my talk that day, alluding to the role that populism played in the campaign and underscored that one must always listen hard to what the people are telling you. After the talk, a person came down from the back row of the large college amphitheater and greeted me at the podium.

It was a young woman. She extended her hand and said, "You all ran an excellent campaign and you should be congratulated." She then did a 180 and walked away before I could say anything. I turned to my host and said, "Did you hear that? That was certainly nice of her." The man said, "It sure was. That was Hillary Rodham."

Surprised and a little shocked, I had no immediate retort, but I couldn't help chuckling to myself a week later when I read a newspaper article that announced that Hillary Rodham had officially changed her name to Hillary Rodham Clinton!

You never know when polling will not only predict the future but also nudge it along.

Chapter 7

Thinking about change:
Candidates and campaigns

The Election of 1980

If you were a Republican in 1980 and that Presidential election was your maiden voyage on the turbulent waters of American politics, then you are sure to remember the main theme of candidate Ronald Reagan's campaign. It was, "Make America Great Again" and launched in the Joe Louis Arena in Detroit, Michigan at the GOP convention.

The one question that has resonated best over the years and has become something of a standard question to voters in every campaign since then is the one Reagan offered in his debate with President Jimmy Carter on October 28, 1980, "Are you better off than you were four years ago?"

This theme was a challenger's dream, especially since the answer was inescapably bad considering the nation was smarting under high gasoline prices, high unemployment, high interest rates and sky-high inflation, not to mention a crisis of leadership. Americans were sorely in need of some hope and some solid leadership. They also needed a strong father figure to replace the uninspiring persona of the occupant of 1600 Pennsylvania Avenue.

There was nothing *slam dunk* about the Reagan campaign, however.

As a matter of fact, on October 26th, just a few weeks before Election Day, Gallup did a poll and found Carter leading Reagan by eight points. After Reagan's performance in the October 28th debate with Carter in which he famously turned to the President with a half smile on his face and said, "There you go again," Reagan made up the deficit.

95

Soon, the news networks were saying that the race was "too close to call" and on November 4th just a week later, Reagan won with 50.8% of the vote to Carter's 41.0% (Independent candidate Congressman John Anderson pulled 6.6% of the vote). While popular vote totals of 43,903,230 votes for Reagan to Carter's 35,480,115 showed a solid 8.4 million vote lead, the real shocker was the imbalance in the electoral vote.

Reagan amassed 489 and Carter only 49. Carter's extremely poor showing by winning only a little over 9% of the electoral votes by taking only the states of Georgia, Hawaii, Maryland, Minnesota, Rhode Island, West Virginia and the District of Columbia was a wake-up call for Democrats all over the country.

Ironically, it was the primary campaigns for both parties that provided most of the interesting fuel to the election fire. There were the George H.W. Bush and John Connally primary challenges on the Rs' side and the Ted Kennedy challenge on the Ds'.

Both parties experienced a temporary schism of sorts with different factions lining up behind their men until the nominations were finally made and accepted. The healing process for the Dems may have been a bit harder than for the Republicans. The reason is that many of them believed 1980 was THE breakthrough year for Kennedy. Kennedy felt the same way and refused to give up without a fight on the convention floor even though Carter came to the convention after winning 24 out of 34 primaries with about 60% of the delegates pledged to him on the first ballot!

The Republicans quickly closed ranks after Reagan won his party's nomination on the first round over his rival, George H.W. Bush, and then closed the remaining gap by tapping Bush to be his Vice-President running mate.

The two campaigns were very different when it came to television advertising. Reagan's ads were often described by those in the media as 'uninspiring,' but not so the man himself. He read his lines like the consummate actor and communicator he was and exuded trust, confidence and friendliness.

By contrast, the Carter ads were split between positive image ads for Carter as a 'peacemaker' (effectively ignoring the bad U.S. economy) and those especially critical of Reagan as a man who could not be trusted.

A commercial shot in Reagan's home state of California showed man-on-the-street interviews with Democrats who were happy to say how 'dangerous' a man like Reagan would be in the White House. One man, obviously a very savvy voter (or paid actor), voiced his concern on how Reagan would manage the Strategic Arms Limitation Talks, a subject not generally debated by the average citizen.

When comparing these ads of over 30 years ago to those of the 2012 campaign, one gets a very clear impression of how much the tone of American political discourse has changed. The envelope of political civility was barely even touched back then let alone pushed to the limits like it is today.

The election of 2012

To many political observers, the election of 2012 began the day President Obama took office in 2009. No sooner did he take the oath of office then both he and his political machine swung into re-election mode. Campaign offices in Iowa (and elsewhere) stayed open in eager anticipation of his next try for the brass ring of a second term.

His team of strategists meticulously analyzed the voting stats and quickly discovered who put him in office. They immediately made plans to court those same voters for the rematch with the Republicans in 2012 while the President launched a flotilla of non-stop fund-raisers that would continue for four long years.

Campaign promises were studied with a view towards paying back the special interest groups that got him to the White House: young women, college students, labor unions, green energy advocates, anti-military organizations and, of course, government-run healthcare devotees.

Most of his promises were quickly broken (like closing Guantanamo Bay) while others took longer to die. His supporters would blame George Bush for literally everything that went wrong with the American economy while other stalwart Democrats would 'play the race card' and say that anyone who opposed Barack Obama obviously had racial motives for doing so.

The 'birthers' with their incessant claims that the President was illegitimately elected (purportedly born on foreign soil), busily stoked the fires of the liberals who quickly labeled ALL Republicans as bigots, idiots and obstructionists.

Then came the Tea Party, and Democrats saw the rise of this movement as a gift from the heavens, enabling them to point their long fingers at the 'whackos' and 'racists' who marched on the nation's Capitol and other venues. (By comparison, the 'Occupy Wall Street' movement earned no real criticism from the White House for its law-breaking.)

America heard a giant, "I told you so" not only from the DNC and its acerbic Chairman and Congresswoman Debbie Wasserman Schultz, but also from countless Obama surrogates and the mainstream media who did their level best to paint hundreds of thousands of ordinary Americans as somehow *unpatriotic* for expressing their displeasure at the way the President was running things.

No Democrat could understand why the 'mandate to govern' (no matter that a 52% marginal win hardly qualified as a mandate) would not be respected. Why were those Republicans doing this? The thought apparently never crossed their mind that reaching across the aisle and engaging Republicans might shed some light on why the opposition was so large and vocal.

The years dragged on, and one giant Presidential promise was realized (the Patients' Affordable Healthcare Act aka Obamacare), passing without a single Republican vote. Instead of tackling the really pressing problems of the day that could have made a national healthcare bill a financially-defensible reality in a healthy economy, the President used up all his political capital on what is bound to be the most expensive piece of legislation in America's history!

Even a college Poli-Sci major could have told the White House that poking a stick in the eye of the opposition so early in his presidency would be a critical error of judgment and only cause the Republicans to dig in and go to DEFCON 4. But that was not Obama's style. The wind was at his back and the *Force* was with him.

What he got for his intransigence was a powerful Republican win in the mid-term election of 2010 as the electorate pushed back, sending him a strong message that they were mad as hell and weren't going to take it anymore. It is times like these that the Founding Fathers must have been pointing their fingers up through their graves saying, "See, that's what we mean by checks and balances!"

99

The gloves were off, and Republicans knew that they needed to at least slow down if not stop the Obama train before it derailed the entire country. Candidates began taking trips to Iowa and New Hampshire and testing the waters for a possible run. The field was crowded, but that didn't seem to bother the Republicans because they were getting more 'face time' with the American voter.

The problem was that the Democrats had already devised 'take down' strategies for each of the Rs' candidates. Santorum was too religious and an enemy of women. Bachmann was off the grid. Gingrich was a has-been. Cain was a one-note samba (9-9-9). Paul was just 'out there' and too fringe. Huntsman was smart but with no apparent following so they left him alone. And Romney, well Romney was a rich capitalist and an enemy of the middle class, plus he was a flip-flopper on healthcare and spending.

The Obama people always knew that Romney would get the Republican nod and they were ready for him long before the primaries began.

They knew him almost as well as he knew himself. Their strategy was to discredit and demean him, show him to be a capitalist wolf in middle-American sheep's clothing and never let up. They marshaled all their forces in each and every city and state.

The talking points of Wall St. vulture/vampire were repeated ad nauseam while the 'knee-breakers' - the Chicago brass knuckle specialists of the upper echelon of the Obama machine - made sure that every prominent Democrat Congressman and Senator spread the word to all the talk shows that Romney, like George H.W. Bush at the supermarket scanner, was 'out of touch' with the common man. The Republican primary debates were a real double-edged sword.

Yes, they did give Republicans more face time, but they also showed the Party's *disarray* (as the Democrats would trumpet) instead of what they really were, an exercise in diversity.

Republicans would counter that it showed the openness of the party and the willingness of the party to engage its leaders in an honest public debate. Unfortunately, the Republicans underestimated the attention-span of the average voter and the brain-washing damage already done by the Democrats.

There were simply too many debates and the public had too much time to see the Party's differences of opinion. The Democrats equated this with a party that didn't have its act together and was wildly flopping around like a flounder on a boat deck. Differences in the party's ideology on family values, abortion, homosexual marriage, tax policy, etc. might have been good TV but it was bad for a party that wanted to unseat a popular rival.

In the end, after spending record sums of money and leaving the ring bruised by his fellow Republicans, Mitt Romney emerged victorious. That was all the Dems needed. The *attack Romney* order was given and the long knives were immediately drawn. Anything Romney ever did or said or wrote or bought or invested in was examined under an electron microscope. Even the car elevator installed in his new home was 'proof' he was an elitist no matter it was for the convenience of his wife who suffers from Multiple Sclerosis.

The micro-campaign strategies were rolled out, and there was a separate message crafted to appeal to literally every voter segment. Single women were warned about losing their abortion rights and their contraceptives thanks to the harangues of a media-hungry Georgetown University student, Sandra Fluke.

Basically the pitch was, "Romney couldn't be trusted. He will take away your birth control and leave you penniless in the streets by dismantling the social safety net and reversing Obamacare!"

Specific appeals to other voter groups like labor unions were also made: "Romney is a union-buster. He'll reverse all the gains made in the last 40 years." The SEIU and the teamsters pummeled their members with fear mongering. Even putting a young, bright and articulate Congressman, Paul Ryan, on the ticket didn't repel the attacks. The Romney campaign had come to a gunfight brandishing a switchblade.

The Presidential and Vice-Presidential debates revealed the extent to which the mainstream media was in the tank for the Democrats. CNN lived up to its reputation as the mainstream liberals' network with the self-insertion by the moderator in defending the President IN THE DEBATE!

In the VP debate, the inane and somewhat bizarre chronic smile-offensive of Vice-President Biden seemed like an attempt to take the audience back to Ronald Reagan's dismissal of President Carter ("There you go again"). While the Vice-President may be a master at some forms of politicking, flashing his pearly whites incessantly at every turn earned him only a quizzical look from Paul Ryan rather than throwing the Congressman off balance. It was just surreal. VP Joe knew he didn't have to hit a home run that night, but he swung hard anyway. The result was he just barely managed to get on base. Most called the debate a tie.

There it was. The stage was set for the President's win. Eventually, 'the big lie' became indistinguishable from reality and the President brought home the bacon with a 52 to 48 victory.

How Republicans can win in a changing America

Themes from the 1980 campaign

Most campaigns bear the fingerprints of the candidate, but in some, the vision of the Party stands out in bold relief. In 1980, once the Republican ticket was chosen, the path forward for the Rs and their campaign was clear. Reagan and Bush (R&B) would project an image of strength to counter the perceived weakness of Jimmy Carter. While R&B certainly had no trouble in mustering up an amiable folksiness when it suited them (especially Reagan), their campaign focused in a businesslike manner on Carter's overall mismanagement of his job.

He was portrayed as ineffectual on the economy, weak on the Iranian hostage crisis and just about everything else except for the Palestinian/Israeli peace talks (which the Republicans left alone). Carter's own folksiness was real and just what you'd expect of a genteel southerner, but it wasn't enough to turn the tide.

Southerners know best that a slow drawl is not synonymous with a slow wit, but the build-up of a little too much *down-homing* on the Presidential scene from the likes of his eccentric brother Billy and even Carter's mother Miss Lillian (who was anything but a shrinking violet) did little to dissuade southern-savvy voters from concluding that *Jimmuh* should be returned from whence he came, to the peanut fields of Plains, Georgia.

R&B ads were low key and precursors of the, 'It's morning in America' TV spots that would come later in the R&B 2.0 campaign. They attempted to win over voters from Blue states without hyperbole, stressing Reagan's accomplishments as Governor in California, saying that when he came into office there was a $194 million deficit and when he left there was a $550 million surplus.

103

For Americans who had been suffering through the oil crisis, high inflation and high unemployment, comforting words coupled with the reminder of such a significant accomplishment were Manna from Heaven for the Reagan campaign and enough for many voters to seriously ponder the question, "Are you better off than four years ago" which Reagan would pose later on.

R&B also used Carter's own 'fireside chats' against him.

(These were reminiscent of FDR's fireside radio chats (1933-1944) which were used to bolster Americans' confidence during the Depression and WWII.)

Carter's brand was the political equivalent of *Mister Rogers*. He was seen cardigan-sweatered near an open hearth speaking in measured quiet tones about America's need to buck up and conserve energy by turning down the thermostat. His famous 'misery index' remarks about President Ford also came home to roost with him in 1980 when his own misery index measured 20 under his presidency, setting a new high-water mark!

The R&B campaign oozed 'older generation' (read: the 'Greatest Generation' as Tom Brokaw called the WWII generation) and with it stability, maturity, wisdom, empathy, honor and duty. Not needing to hammer Carter with something that was evident for all to see, the campaign instead decided to present their team as an acceptable alternative.

Democrat strategists knew that the 1980 campaign would be a test of ideology AND pragmatism. They attempted to gird their loins with spots that spoke about Reagan's superficiality, his untested decision-making skills and his unpredictability under pressure.

How Republicans can win in a changing America

Their commercials included ones underscoring the President's military record (Jimmy Carter: A military man and a man of peace), his peacemaker image (the 'nobility of peace') and a man of religious faith (the 'bible' spot). They attempted to capture the high road, but didn't realize that they first had to pass Reagan to even get on the on-ramp.

Themes from the 2012 campaign

No matter how much political scientists, consultants, pundits and politi-geeks tried to spin it, the Democratic Party's political campaign of 2012 seemed like an uncomfortable pairing of two Hollywood movies: the aggressiveness of the *Gangs of New York* and the otherworldliness of *Dr. Strangelove*.

There was nothing high-brow or sophisticated about the Democrats' tone or its tactics. It was a bare-knuckled assault on the Republican Party, its platform, its values and its candidate, Mitt Romney. Theirs was not an iron hand in a velvet glove; it was an all-out, no holds barred attempt to search and destroy the Republicans with a scorched earth onslaught.

The Rs never knew what hit them. While they were playing a version of the Reagan *shining city on a hill* card in an attempt to take the civil moral high ground, the Dems had suited up in full riot gear and took to the airwaves and the streets with dire warnings that a Republican win would turn America into a rich versus poor nation where greedy capitalists, homophobes, woman-haters and racists would rule.

The Rs assumed (incorrectly) that such an approach would fail because of the inherent goodness, fairness and intelligence of the American electorate. How wrong they were.

How Republicans can win in a changing America

Had they done their homework, they would have known that our deteriorating economic condition was successfully blamed on the Republicans (and the do-nothing Congress) by the Dems instead of where it belonged...at the doorstep of an inept tone-deaf Administration and a divisive President.

The Obama machine waged a multi-front war as it picked specific voter groups and tailored individual messages to each of them. There was the 'values' argument where the Rs would overturn Roe vs. Wade, forbid contraception to needy women (the Fluke argument) and reduce women to chattel, effectively turning back the clock to pre-woman's suffrage movement days.

The Dems found their usual supporters from the ranks of the non-profits, womens' groups and of course a willing media. They mined the emotions of the urban poor and specific racial and ethnic groups convincing them that, as Vice-President Biden said, "They (sic, the Rs) would put you all back in chains." The most vulnerable target was those greedy rich Americans who had, as the President said, "...not built that" (referring to their achievements) and thereby laid the groundwork for a multitude of specialized attacks based on a false accusation that somehow American business' economic success was unfair, lopsided and didn't reflect an equitable distribution of wealth (the Obama fairness doctrine).

It was an easy connection to make, especially if one only looked at the stock market and the "trillions of dollars that American companies were hoarding on the sidelines." This message resonated with America's working poor who saw their home values and 401Ks (if they had one) drop precipitously while energy and food prices rose at the same time that America's companies were *turning a blind eye* to their situation.

Unfortunately, the Rs didn't counter the argument forcefully enough, though they did try to place the blame squarely where it belonged...on reckless government spending, failed stimulus packages, indefensible lending to flawed companies like Solyndra and Fisker, to name but two disastrous investments.

This segued neatly into the Democrat thesis that Republicans were against 'infrastructure investment' (read: education, research and development and WPA-like projects) that would have put thousands of Americans back to work. No 'shining city on a hill' metaphor could compete with this kind of hardball messaging.

Republicans lost the argument because they didn't make a clear cause and effect connection between economic growth and a proven private sector empowerment model.

Instead, the electorate saw the Republicans painted as opposing a government-funded Democrat-led 'recovery.' Democrats proposed that a continuance of the ARRA (stimulus) package, or more government spending and indebtedness, was the only sound way to turn around states' dwindling fortunes and reverse the increasing and highly worrisome unemployment stats. It made no difference that this approach failed miserably in creating sustainable employment during Obama 1.0. Market-based solutions were portrayed as unworkable and nothing more than corporate welfare.

The Democrats used sleight of hand and created a diversion from the real problems of an economy on the skids just as they did in the Carter campaign of 1980, but this time the strategy worked. The Romney resumé, charm offensive and appeal to the better angels of Americans' nature were not strong enough to counter the Democrats' class warfare.

How Republicans can win in a changing America

The kill shot came when a video surfaced of Mitt Romney speaking at a private fund-raiser where he was recorded as saying that would not count on 47% of the electorate to vote for him.

This was proof enough that Republicans didn't care a whit about the disadvantaged, the poor and the unemployed, and Democrats went to town with it, quoting Romney's 47% statement to anyone who would listen.

Savvy political consultants could have turned this around and spoken about the 47% as an important American voter group and made the case for helping them rise above their circumstances with help from a compassionate Republican Party with good ideas, but they didn't. Embarrassment left them frozen in place, paralyzed and without an adequate defense...or offense.

Chapter 8

Thinking about change:
The new media

The Electronic Doorstep: We're livin' in a whole nuther time, one that is punctuated by enormous speed and breathtaking brevity. A rumor, accusation or downright lie needn't wait to be set in type or be loaded into a TV anchor's teleprompter.

These days you can get your dirt delivered right to your mobile phone or tablet computer an instant after it's sent by some blogger sitting in a darkened corner of his basement or political activist who's just uploaded a YouTube video of an Occupy Wall Street protest.

Proponents will say, "Great." Cynics will say, "Heaven forbid they should have to wait a day to corroborate their sources' allegations and then have to pull the story." If you're one of the latter, you're among the few, the proud and the brave of the enlightened electorate. The bald truth is, however, that salaciousness sells. Just ask the likes of Anthony Weiner, Elliot Spitzer or Mark Sanford.

Managing the message and doing damage control is a 24/7 job and it's not for the technology-challenged campaign or party. Bad news arrives almost before it's left the sender's keyboard, hell bent on toppling the unsuspecting candidate.

Truth is, we're at a place in time when the quest for truth is often an afterthought and not a guiding principle. We can bemoan it, regret it and even be sad about it, but we can't ignore it. If you don't 'tweet' or 'friend' someone, you're probably way over 30 and still write *thank you* cards to your friends. Nothing wrong with that, mind you. You had just better hope that the leaders in your party understand the importance of the new social media and are using it to communicate with the youthful voter.

How Republicans can win in a changing America

What are these new media and how do they work?

Picture the old chain letter and how you used to send it on to your friends. You took great pains to copy it, fold it, plop it into an envelope, seal and stamp it and then hopped on your bike and delivered it to the post office.

Today, you supercopy somebody else's message, log on to your social media account and upload it to your Facebook page. Presto! You're an electronic messenger, a high-tech Paul Revere. Your message is now in the hands of everybody who is one of your 'friends' or is linked to your page.

You could also upload that message as part of a thread onto a pundit's site like the Daily Kos or the Huffington Post and wait for the 'sniffer bots' of the major search engines to find an interesting combination of words in it and then throw it up on the Internet for all to find. Congratulations, your message now has the potential to be seen by literally tens of millions of people the world over.

Let's recap. That remark you made about the candidate's cruelty to his household pets has now circled the globe. People in the remotest regions of the planet are now busy relaying that message via their email accounts, giving even wider distribution to your accusations. Soon the mainstream media will carry the story, completing the circle of smear and the ASPCA will soon be banging on your candidate's door.

The bottom line is, it should have never gotten this far. The Republican Party's social media masters must develop strategies to defuse, short-circuit or combat these kinds of messages, preferably before they reach the ether. That brings us to the so-called *mainstream media* and their passionate sophomoric man crush on President Barack Obama.

111

Whole books have been written on this subject. One, "A Slobbering Love Affair" by author Bernie Goldberg, laid out the case quite well on why so many in the media chose to jettison their objectivity and become the official White House lap dog for President Obama, his administration and its policies. Again, it will do no good for us to long for those thrilling days of yesteryear when truth, justice and the American way were not simply words from a Superman episode intro but real guiding principles.

The Daily Planet has morphed into the Daily Pundit. Respectable and responsible news-gathering has become yesterday's news. It has been replaced by a tabloid mentality, complete with tabloid journalists who are more interested in sound bites or a clever bit of innuendo rather than fair and balanced reporting.

Instances of downright yellow journalism are everywhere, and as we said, whole books have chronicled them, so we won't go into them here. Decent Americans deserve a better more impartial press not the one that calls itself the fourth estate today. But what can decent Americans DO about it?

The answers and the choices are really pretty simple.

They come down to two courses of action, each requiring some engagement and commitment on our part. The first option is to cancel our subscriptions to the offending newspapers or cable channels. While the 'that'll show them' approach will have an effect, it will only be a temporary one. Better to take the road less traveled and use our First Amendment right of free speech and free expression against the very institutions that are supposed to be protecting it. Yes, we're referring to letter-to-the-editor-writing, emailing and telephone calling.

A constant barrage of reasoned, pointed citizen push-back will have an effect. It may take time, but eventually an unbalanced medium can be righted through the power of the pen. It's possible that this very act of pushing back could shake some of the media loose from their barnacles, make them more interesting to follow AND ultimately help them recover from their downward slide towards economic insolvency.

Getting the media to take back their class ring from President Obama is another challenge altogether.

Surveys conducted of TV journalists have revealed that a significant percentage of them self-identify with the Democratic Party. Convincing them to keep their politically-colored opinions to themselves is considerably easier said than done. However, we can all become the media's copy editors and question their choice of stories and their use of certain words and phrases that reveal their political bias.

A case in point...

In 2013, the Senate Minority Leader, Senator Mitch McConnell of Kentucky, was having a meeting with his re-election campaign staff. They were discussing simple opposition research (this was not a 'dirty-tricks' Nixonian operation) on a potential challenger for Senator McConnell's seat.

A political activist group made a surreptitious audio recording of the meeting and gave it to a left-wing blog. It was promptly sling-shotted to the outermost regions of the Internet where it was heard by hundreds of thousands if not millions of people. The recording was vivid in detail about how the McConnell campaign would counter the potential challenger's campaign by using public domain information on her (a common campaign strategy).

113

THIS is the story the media decided to write, NOT the more insidious story of how the meeting in the campaign office might have been illegally recorded - a <u>crime</u>.

<u>That</u> choice - of which story to run - actually reveals how the media colludes with itself, from the writer to the editor and back to the writer. A politically-biased journalist would never be able to get his politically-biased story in print without the go-ahead from a politically-biased editor. It follows then that none of their decisions could have been made without a politically-biased publisher supported by a politically-biased board and/or investors.

If we want to change the paradigm to one rooted in fairness, where both stories (the McConnell opposition research story and the bugging story) compete equally for the *ink*, we will need to resort to determined activism. Individual readers, many individual readers, must call out bias whenever they see it or hear it no matter how tedious and repetitive the task might be. A well-organized party communication apparatus can certainly help blow journalists' cover and reveal their true identities by carefully monitoring their copy, but the real power lies with the reader and viewer.

The generation gap

"Never trust anyone over thirty" was the popular expression of the sixties and even seventies. An updated version of that might be, "Never trust anyone, especially politicians." Trust and respect used to go hand in hand and were two things our public institutions expected and got from us. In the 80s, under President Reagan, we trusted but verified (at least when it came to the Soviet Union).

114

In the first two decades of the new millennium, we Americans have lost most of our trust in our leaders, our institutions and even ourselves. While it may be convenient to ascribe this lack of trust to a new generation of young Americans (a typical attitude of older generations), we do not believe that the younger generation is the Bermuda Triangle of America's trust. Social scientists will probably differ on the root causes of why we view our leaders with cynicism, disdain and skepticism, but common sense supplies at least some of the answers.

Loyalty and trust are two gifts we reserve for people who tell us the truth, who lead by example and who keep their promises. It is, therefore, no wonder that after several political sex scandals, blatant deceit on the part of several Presidents, cover-ups and broken promises, that the American electorate holds its leaders in such low regard.

While President Obama's approval rating as of this writing is under 50% (actually under 35% for his handling of the economy), Congress' approval rating hovers around 14%! By 2013, our Democrat-controlled Senate had not produced a budget in four years. The President's own 2014 budget was 60 days late and contained an unworkable combination of tax increases and miniscule spending cuts (actually cuts in the rate of spending growth).

One of these was the re-figuring of the Consumer Price Index as it related to automatic Social Security increases. By introducing this, the President broke his own promise, one he made in 2008 while campaigning for office...not to hurt seniors. A four-year long war against America's business sector and America's job creators waged by the President and his men took its toll as millions still remained unemployed even after trillion dollar plus TARP and ARRA *stimulus* packages failed.

115

Millions more Americans simply stopped looking for work and made our labor participation rate the worst since the Great Depression. America's youth noticed, too, as their resumes couldn't even get them inside corporate America's doors for an interview!

Many of <u>them</u> stopped looking for work and did a u-turn back to the safety of the halls of ivy hoping to find temporary shelter from the worst economic storm their generation had ever seen. No one can blame our youth for being naive or for lacking experience. Life takes care of that over time, but do we have the time to wait?

The gap we feel with our children and grandchildren is part of an evolutionary process that occurs quite naturally from one generation to another. The difference this time is the immediate need to close that gap so that we can gain our youth's solidarity in righting our ship of state. We must be willing to make a concerted effort to understand them; to talk to them about the issues and the consequences of voting for style over substance; and to help them understand us and why we support conservative principles.

Back in 1970, the cartoonist Walt Kelly who drew the famous comic strip character Pogo had him say, "We have met the enemy and he is us," and there was a great deal of truth to it. The 70s were a tumultuous time that pushed Americans to opposite corners of the political spectrum and created a generation gap as big as the Grand Canyon.

The enemy is always us, or rather it is us in the guise of our inability to bridge a divide, understand the other guy's opinion or meet on neutral ground.

That goes double for our children. If we want our children to become politically active, we must take an active role in their education at an early stage, otherwise we will leave them in the hands of the Bill Ayres, Ward Churchills, Saul Alinskys and the thousands of secular Progressive professors of America's universities who will, happily, indoctrinate them for us.

The education process begins at home, and how it is conducted is important. If our children see us rant and rave at the television set every time we hear something that upsets us, we will be endorsing loud and uncivil speech instead of calm and reasoned debate. In generations past, school and home were better connected to each other and to the world. Teachers encouraged cooperation among parents and their children with something called, *Current Events*.

CE was a home/school assignment where students were encouraged to discuss important world events of the day with their parents and then bring those opinions back into the classroom for a debate. It is programs as innocent as this one that form the nexus between curiosity and knowledge and help to create politically-aware citizens out of the whole cloth of our children. We must also face certain facts about our interaction with America's youth. One of those is the increasing difficulty in making things *interesting* and *exciting* especially when it concerns politics. The other is our hesitancy to adopt new technology as a way of reaching our children.

If we are to be successful in growing human beings with an unstoppable curiosity and skill for finding answers we must take an interest in their lives and debate them not as authority figures but as equal partners on a journey towards their own enlightenment. We may never totally eliminate our political generation gap, but to ignore its existence will only make it bigger and more difficult to close, later.

How Republicans can win in a changing America

Messaging/Matchups

"We won. Get over it." These words were (and still are) slung around by Democratic operatives, Congressmen and Senators as if they would somehow magically trigger an automatic positive response from the Republican losers!

The more moderate surrogates for the DNC simply said, "Elections have consequences" implying that like young girls in Victorian times, who when faced with the inevitable consummation of their marriages should just, "close your eyes and think of England." No one gains any purchase from trying to make the loser a willing supplicant to the victor's ideology. Surrendering our right of future opposition is another.

Republicans are still walking around in lock-step like zombies in a video by Michael Jackson - stuck in total disbelief that a man of such talent and intelligence like Mitt Romney would be bested by an amateur like Barack Obama.

The Ds are right; we must 'get over it,' BUT more importantly, we must 'get on with it.'

How Republicans can win in a changing America

Chapter 9

Lessons on winning:
The language of elections

Words matter...

especially those that are crafted for a political campaign. The messenger matters, too, whether it's the candidate himself, his surrogates, the man on the street, the poor or down-trodden or those viewed as doing the down-trodding.

Americans were still reasonably polite in 1980. This is surprising given the enormous challenges that faced the country like an abysmal economy, the Cold War, cultural unrest and the fissures that were appearing in literally all areas of our society. While some of our insecurity was due to ordinary generational change, other factors contributed significantly to our identity crisis.

We were feeling small and powerless thanks to the Iranian hostage crisis (adding to the injury our pride suffered during the Vietnam War years). We were rudderless, adrift in an angry economic sea with no calm skies in sight and more importantly, with no competent captain at the helm.

The Carter campaign strategists knew that words alone would not sell Americans on giving Carter another four years so they decided to court the largest voter demographic that would respond to a pitch for reason and for staying the course.

This was the same demographic that the Rs were courting - the mature over-40 American voter - and by doing so nearly ignored the younger voter. The 'Disco Generation' was left to fend for itself, politically, but sided (at least philosophically) with the Democrats and their 'make peace not war' policy. The Carter campaign rhetoric was heavily laced with words of peace, portraying Carter as a peacemaker, a man of peace and a peaceful and contemplative man not given to snap decisions. The implied message was, of course, that Reagan wasn't any of those things.

How Republicans can win in a changing America

Threading the needle or walking the line between pacifism and power was done in Carter TV commercials by showing aircraft carriers and powerful military images with Carter's voice occasionally heard speaking in measured tones with a narrator offering the President's military record as proof that here was a warrior who knew the power *and price* of peace.

Tone mattered, too. Back in 1980, the low gravelly-voiced 'doomsday' narrator hadn't as yet replaced the straightforward crisp annunciation of the 'advertising narrator,' and this synched up well with the TV spots of the day.

(The man-on-the-street commercial filmed in California to lambaste Reagan could just as well have been hawking toothpaste as Carter for President.)

For many, Vietnam was still a very real experience. It was only seven years since the Paris Peace Accords, and those veterans who weren't in VA hospitals recuperating from debilitating wounds were pounding the pavement unable to find work and wondering why their government hadn't done a better job at finding THEM jobs. While Carter may have been in the military, Reagan exuded *Commander-in-Chief* and veterans responded to his style and posture. It didn't hurt that Reagan's film career was replete with leading man roles, though it's hard to tell how much style influenced substance with veteran's groups back then.

Reagan's words were his foot soldiers, sent out to soften up the enemy and shore up support among his own troops. Speeches were hand-crafted with just the right touch for the right audience. When Reagan looked up we all looked up. When his words painted a picture of an America that we all thought was gone and forgotten, he breathed life into it for us.

121

America was on the cusp of societal change, but a kind of *retro change* that took us back to those thrilling days of yesteryear when men were men and their women were respected and worked right alongside them, carving out a bold future from a raw wilderness.

It may sound corny, but people return to the familiar and safe when frightened. The majority of Americans relived history with Reagan and didn't seem to mind that he was an older man who dyed his hair and spoke like everybody's favorite uncle.

Nothing could be more foreign to each other than the language of the political campaigns of 1980 and 2012. In both speeches and commercials, the 2012 campaign of the Democrats reflected an American society that had suddenly morphed from Gone with the Wind genteel to Girls Gone Wild grotty, so huge was the disparity.

Mitt Romney was portrayed as a cross between mean old capitalist Mister Potter from *It's a wonderful life* and Hannibal Lecter from *Silence of the lambs.* No velvet-throated voice-over here, the tone was Armageddon-like. Political Action Committees (PACs) like Priorities USA served up such gems as the 'Romney's a killer' spot. You remember it don't you? Here's the *translation...*

Bain Capital bought our parent company and then shut down the plant I worked at and I was laid off and then my wife contracted cancer and we didn't have enough insurance to pay for her hospital bills and she died which is why Romney is bad (read: at fault) because Bain Capital is bad because capitalism is bad because the profit motive is bad which is why you should vote for the Democrats.

122

Had there been a category for the spot requiring the most ginormous chutzpah, the greatest suspension of disbelief and the most convoluted logic, this spot would have won the blue ribbon, hands-down.

Romney's spots were aimed at the Obama jugular, but in typical nice-guy fashion they were released like a fast ball and turned into a slider before they found their target, perhaps out of some misguided reverence for the office of the President.

The Democrat strategists must have chuckled over the Rs' attack ads in much the same way Sean Connery's Chicago character in *The Untouchables* did when he surprised a hit man at his door holding a switchblade (Connery's carrying a shotgun) saying, "Isn't that just like a Wop? Brings a knife to a gunfight."

While the comparison is crude and the line hardly flattering to Italians, it is politics 101 in Chicago circles where the game is played the old-fashioned way, bare knuckled with no holds barred. In actuality, the Romney campaign channeled the Reagan campaign perhaps unaware that a third of the voters in the 2012 election probably didn't even remember Ronald Reagan or those more civil times in America's history.

The Dems chuckled at Romney's *squareness* as if he just stepped out of an episode of 'Madmen.' They laughed at the Obama barbs about "Big Bird better watching his step" (Romney wanted to cut PBS funding) and "the only street Romney was intent on cleaning up was Sesame Street."

They continued laughing as comedians like Bill Maher, David Letterman and Jon Stewart pounded away at Romney like shipboard guns targeting the beaches on D-Day.

How Republicans can win in a changing America

When the political history books are written about the words and rhetoric of the 2012 Presidential campaign, they will undoubtedly say that both candidates suited up for the event. The difference was that one was dressed for the opera while the other was clad in SWAT gear wearing his game face.

Chapter 10

Lessons on losing:
Why the right was wrong

T he most dangerous thing a candidate can do...

is ignore his instincts. The most dangerous thing a political party can do is start believing its own public relations. There are many reasons why human beings and organizations fail.

Usually, the reasons can be boiled down to three major ones:

1. we do not seek out the truth
2. we do not thoroughly understand the meaning of the truth
3. we do not act on the truth

The Republican Party's failure to win the Presidency in 2012 was due to all three, plus a couple. The country had four years to wake up from its economic coma and choose a different direction, but it chose to stay the course giving added meaning to Albert Einstein's quote: "Insanity: doing the same thing over and over again and expecting different results."

Mistake #1: Believing that a political party cannot accommodate major change without losing its identity

Even the mighty oak tree bends with the wind, lest it break. To the outside world (the world of non-Republican voters) the right wing of the Party looks like a petrified forest, rigid, calcified and somehow out of touch with modern times.

It appears unfeeling, cold and unforgiving with members who come off as strict constructionists and 'Bible thumpers' who would rob you (if you're an avowed Democrat or Secular Progressive) of your human rights to contraception, abortion, homosexual marriage and would tear down the wall separating church and state and put up a year-round Nativity scene on every public space.

126

The more moderate middle of the Party doesn't look much better because, after all, the left doesn't understand why any party would allow or tolerate 'radicals' like those of the right wing inside it.

Suffering from that association, the moderates of the Party feel squeezed. They pledge the same allegiance to family values, protection of the unborn and fealty to a set of conservative economic principles that the right wing wants, but they're hesitant about going out and proselytizing about it.

In order to accommodate any change be it large or small, you must first create the *conditions* for change, something the Republican Party has had trouble doing. The outside world knows that the Party is fractured, but the inside world of the Party seems oblivious to it. For a real life example, look at the divided opinion in the Catholic church. While church teaching prohibits contraception, many if not most Catholics practice it. While abortion is anathema to the sanctity of life, many Catholics condone it or at least look the other way.

The Republicans' mistake is their fear of losing their identity and their base if they change. What they don't know is that fear can only live in darkness and ignorance. It's time to throw open the shutters and let the sunlight of divergent views in.

Mistake #2: Underestimating the opposition

In the *Art of War* Sun Tzu said, "We are not fit to lead an army on the march unless we are familiar with the face of the country - its mountains and forests, its pitfalls and precipices, its marshes and swamps." Clearly, the Republicans were not familiar with the face of the opposition, the Democratic voter or the steadfast support they gave their candidate despite his blunderings or missteps.

127

Neither did the Rs correctly assess the strength of the Obama forces because they didn't go where Team Obama went.

Again, Sun Tzu: "An army may march great distances without distress, if it marches through country where the enemy is not." The Obama Machine was well-oiled and battle-tested in 2008, and the decision to leave some of it in place (volunteers and paid staff in certain states) during Obama 1.0 helped provide continuity and ensure a rapid response later on in the run-up to Obama 2.0.

Republicans also misjudged the efficacy of Obama surrogates and the willingness of the media to give them airtime. The same is true for the Get out the Vote(r) drives that netted hundreds of thousands of new (largely Democrat) voters. The Rs also underestimated the power of the Democratic Party 'hit squads' (PACs) and the role they would play in destroying the image of Mitt Romney.

Who could forget the 2008 Deputy Campaign Manager, Stephanie Cutter's appearance on television and her assertion that candidate Romney "...could have committed a felony," by saying he wasn't on the Bain Board when SEC documents said he was. This was later trumped by Majority Leader of the Senate, Harry Reid, who said, "So the word is out that he (Romney) has not paid taxes in ten years." Reid added injury to insult by making these comments on the floor of the Senate!

Then there was Mr. Obama himself. While Ronald Reagan may have been the *Teflon President*, Obama was certainly the *Kevlar President*. Nothing could penetrate the shield of bullet-proof rhetoric that emanated from the President, and nothing could keep him off balance for long.

After his poor showing in the second of three Presidential Debates, Obama bounced back and bested Romney (with help from the CNN moderator) in their final encounter. Though many agreed that each won one debate and one was a draw, the one people remembered most was the final debate and that gave the President an advantage.

Mistake #3: Misjudging the electorate

Republicans were convinced that anyone hurt by the Obama Recession would never support him again. This went double for small business owners, defenders of the Constitution and lovers of liberty. Imagine their shock at learning that their base didn't turn out as they expected and that their man lost by three million votes!

Upon closer inspection, the Rs' shock turned to disbelief when the numbers were run and it was evident that young single women, Blacks and Hispanic voters had showed up in force, trouncing the Romney supporters. The American electorate had clearly changed. No longer could the Republicans count on common sense and logic (and their base) to conquer emotion and charisma.

Analyses of all sorts are in the works in preparation for the Congressional and Senate races in 2014, so it's too early to say what exactly is motivating the Democratic voters to ignore the reality of a failed Obama economic policy, a divisive social policy, a flawed energy policy and an amateurish foreign policy.

We can only hope that Republicans are able to regroup, rethink and re-insert themselves into America's political consciousness and present reasonable alternatives to the Democrat candidates for the House and Senate. If they don't, they will surely lose the

How Republicans can win in a changing America

House and end up where they began in 2008, only this time the results will be catastrophic for their policies.

Mistake #4: The organization that wasn't

If there is one overarching mistake the Republicans made (and may still be making) it is the undervaluing of what a tight-knit, effective organization comprised of dedicated people who are willing to sweat blood for their candidate can mean to winning elections.

The Democrats' organization was superior. There's no getting around it. Unless Republicans are willing to invest the time and money necessary in developing one that can plan wisely, strategize cleverly, communicate professionally, think on its feet and respond rapidly, it will continue to lose when pitted against the Democrats' *Machine*. Though it may sound heretical to some Republicans looking for a clear path forward, it might be wise to heed Sun Tzu's words: "All war is based on deception."

The ones we must never deceive or delude, however, is ourselves.

Chapter 11

Lessons on winning:
Follow the money

For nearly two centuries...

Americans have financed their Presidential election campaigns with a tangled mix of private contributions that were largely unregulated and below the radar screen of the average citizen. That situation existed until 1971 when Congress passed the Federal Election Campaign Act (FECA) and the Revenue Act (RA). The FECA required candidates to report their expenses and contributions and the RA set up a Presidential Election Campaign Fund that candidates could use.

The money for the fund came from U.S. Taxpayers who could check off an optional box on their income tax returns that diverted $1.00 (now $3.00) from the U.S. Treasury to the fund. By agreeing to use the fund to finance their campaigns, candidates could draw down lump sums of taxpayer dollars to cover general election-related expenses with the provision that they could not accept private donations or spend money raised for primary contests.

Later, in 1975, Congress amended the FECA to limit individual contributions and provide matching funds on small donations to primary candidates. That same legislation set up the new Federal Election Commission (www.fec.gov) which would administer and enforce the act. Since then, candidates have been permitted to take a limited amount of federal funds (set by the FEC) and use them in primary contests, albeit under the careful scrutiny of the FEC.

Current members of the FEC are: Ellen L. Weintraub, Chair Donald F. McGahn, Vice-Chair, Carolyn C. Hunter, Matthew S. Peterson, and Steven T. Walther (Commissioners). All were appointed by the President and confirmed by the Senate.

How Republicans can win in a changing America

Campaign costs have been rising dramatically since the FECA was passed, and it wasn't always easy for candidates to husband these resources and stretch them out to cover all the primaries. This was true of Bob Dole's campaign in 1996, for example.

Candidates have found these funds to be insufficient to mount primary contests. Several candidates opted out like George W. Bush did in 2000 (though he did accept $67.6 million in general election public funds). Both Howard Dean and John Kerry said 'no' to public funds for their primary contests

In the 2008 election, Barack Obama changed his position on accepting public funds (he was for it before he was against it) fearing he would not be able to adequately defend himself against what his campaign felt would be an onslaught of ads by '527' groups, (named for a section of the tax code) the same kinds of largely unregulated groups of private individuals that did in John Kerry in 2004.

Upon hearing this, Senator John McCain of Arizona said, about Senator Obama, that he "has completely reversed himself and gone back, not on his word to me, but the commitment he made to the American people."

Had Obama accepted public funds he would have only gotten about $84 million for the general election; his people knew he could raise much more from private contributors.

Many political strategists and insiders suspected the Obama Machine would take this decision, but McCain bought himself a few minutes of the high ground with his quote and laid down a marker on one of the first of many campaign promises that candidate Obama would break.

Enter the election and campaigns of 2012

To quote the Beatles, "Money can't buy me love," but it sure can buy you the White House.

The record-breaking extravaganza called the election contest of 2012 was hyped more than the *Thrilla in Manilla*, the launch of the iphone and *Who killed J.R.*, combined.

It pitted a man who not only felt your pain (and said he would relieve you of it) against a man who was purported to *cause* pain by breaking up companies and relieve you of your future. Such was the excess of the estimated nearly $6.0 billion spent on the election in total and the $2.0 billion raised for spending by the campaigns. It all bordered on the obscene, especially at a time when many Americans were losing their homes and livelihood. How could we let this happen?

The most expensive election campaigns in history

In 1980, candidates Carter and Reagan each received $29.4 million in campaign money from the Federal coffers. That was their limit, and they were forbidden to spend any more (Reagan ended up spending $29.2 million while Carter spent it all). Each bought about $15 million worth of television ads.

Today, that's considered 'chump change' and was eclipsed in 2012 by an estimated over $2.0 billion dollars raised and spent by both the Obama and Romney campaigns (and their Superpacs). The estimate is that the Obama campaign raised about $1.2 billion while the Romney camp raised slightly under $1.0 billion. It is believed that each campaign still has millions of dollars in unspent funds.

By law, that money (minus payments for any debts) may be used to finance future campaigns for the same candidate or be given to charities and/or state and local candidates for their campaigns. For the Democrats (since Obama cannot run again), the money would have to be transferred to the DNC for their use for a future candidate or, as with the Republicans, it could be given to charities and/or state and local party candidates. According to the FEC Guide, the money could also be refunded to donors. Think that will happen?

How did we go from $60 million in 1980 to over $2.0 billion in 2012?

Campaign costs have exploded in recent decades. Airtime for 30 and 60 second TV spots has increased markedly as have the costs to produce those spots (think Broadway versus off-Broadway). The price of consultants, campaign staffs, travel, accommodations, venue costs, printing, communications, polling, etc. have also skyrocketed since 1980. Then there's the perceived need on the part of the campaign consultants to carpet bomb the voters with incessant messages that will, they hope, seep into their consciousness and win their vote.

The PACs

Without campaign support from Political Action Committees (PACs), and now Super PACs, candidates would have to sling their own mud from the low road instead of traveling the safety of the unassailable political high road while others do it for them. PACs were first organized in the 1940s, and the one formed by the CIO (Congress of Industrial Organizations - later to become partnered with the American Federation of Labor or AFL) in 1943 became the model for other successive PACs to follow.

Thirty years later, PACs became more regulated with limits placed on individual contributions, but the Supreme Court ruling in 2010 (the *Citizens United* case) ended restrictions on their funding and gave greater latitude for corporate giving as well.

Most PACs represent special interest groups and coalitions while some Super PACs (offshoots of PACs but ones that typically seek larger unlimited donations) are directly aligned with individual political campaigns like Priorities USA Action for the Democrats and Restore Our Future for the Republicans.

Each played a pivotal role in the 2012 election. For example, Priorities USA Action collected just over $65 million and spent 100% of it 'attacking Mitt Romney.' Not to be outdone, Restore Our Future took in approx. $145 million and spent 87% 'attacking Barack Obama' and 13% 'supporting Mitt Romney.'

The top ten contributors to Restore Our Future were: Sheldon Adelson (Casino owner) $10 mill.; Miriam Adelson (Physician and wife of Sheldon Adelson) $20 mill.; Bob J. Perry (Houston homebuilder) $10 mil.; Oxbow Carbon LLC (Oil and gas company in W. Palm Beach, FL) $2.8 mill.; Harold Simmons (Dallas, TX billionaire) $2.3 mill.; Julian Robertson (Founder of Tiger Management hedge fund) $2.2 mill.; Robert Reynolds (CEO, Putman Investments) $1.6 mill.; Kenneth C. Griffin (Founder and CEO of Citadel LLC) $1.6 mill.; A. Jerrold Perenchio (Billionaire and former CEO of Univision) $1.5 mill. and Stanley Herzog (Chairman/CEO of Herzog Contracting) $1.2 million.

The top ten contributors to Priorities USA Action were: Fred Eychaner (an Obama bundler and Chicago media mogul) $3.5 mill.; James H. Simons (President of Euclid Capital and Board Chair of Renaissance Technologies corp., a hedge fund company) $3.5 mill.; Jeffrey Katzenberg (CEO of Dreamworks Animation) $3.0 mill.; United Assoc. of Journeymen and Apprentices of the

Pipe fitting Industry (Labor Union) $2.0 mill.; Irwin Jacobs (Founder of Qualcomm and former MIT professor) $2.0 mill.; Jon Stryker (founder Arcus Foundation) $2.0 mill.; Steve Mostyn (Texas trial lawyer) $2.0 mill.; Ann Cox Chambers (Part owner of Cox Enterprises, a media conglomerate) $2.0 mill.; Ann Wyckoff (Seattle philanthropist) $1.5 mill. and Natl. Air Traffic Controllers Association PAC (PAC of Air Traffic Controllers labor union) $1.2 million.

(Source: New York Times, Election 2012)

And the winner is?

Answer: The American economy, or rather a select part of the American economy. The first beneficiary is the media. Then come the venue owners, leasing companies, bus operators, hotels and motels, the airlines, restaurants, souvenir manufacturers, printers. The list goes on and on. In fact, elections are good for our economy and, did we mention, democracy and of course, the candidates?

The only thing that would be better for our economy would be a large foreign investor who would bankroll the entire shebang. Obviously, that person or entity could not have any business pending before the U.S. Government or know anybody in the Government or the House or the Senate or Lobbyists (just to keep things on the up and up).

And the likelihood of that happening is? Zero. So we must face facts; no candidate will ever take a bite of the Federal Campaign Financing apple again, not as long as it takes a billion dollars to get that $400K/year job of Commander-in-Chief. Republicans must take up the issue of campaign reform and view it as a high priority item. Our elections are important to our democracy.

They should not be treated like 'Dancing with the Stars' on steroids. What kind of candidates will we get for our money if we don't? The rich and famous, celebrities, cult figures, lottery winners? We need serious people for this most serious of top jobs and that goes for other races like Congress and the Senate, too. Republicans must speak with the voice of reason even if they have to take it down from the shelf and re-tune it.

Chapter 12

America's migration:
Red vs. Blue states

"The Republican Party is your parents' party.

The Democratic Party is your party. Red is dead; Blue is true." If we allow these sentiments to prevail, we might as well reserve a spot for our party in a glass-enclosed diorama at the Smithsonian Institution. THAT's how important the 2014 election is.

The Democrats won in 2012 by demagoguery and by denigrating and demoralizing the opposition in Red, Blue and Purple states. There were only minimal alterations made to their message to accommodate local issues (like labor union support, for example) while they hammered away at everything else very early on. Their brilliance showed through in a decision to leave certain campaign offices and staff in place for four years in states like Iowa.

Classic Roman tactics of divide and conquer worked. Swing states swung their way not because of re-districting but because of active get out the vote(r) drives coupled with early and better messaging. Like the successful martial arts practitioner, the Democrats used Republicans' 'body mass' (gaffes, unchallenged accusations and innuendo) against them.

Why are the Blue states Blue and the Red states Red?

On average, Americans used to pick up stakes and move households every seven years. These days, our mobility has been severely curtailed because of a lackluster economy and dramatically reduced home prices/values. In short, we can't afford it no matter how cheap the U-Haul is. The exodus from North to South (rust belt to sun belt) that started decades ago has slowed and has not as yet been overtaken by a West to near

140

West to Southeast shift as the California economy, for example, spirals downward. While countless Californians have packed up and shipped out, the state is still very much in the Blue column. Its expats, however, are adding to the Democrat rolls in not only other Blue states but also several Red and Purple states.

Many solid Blue states remain Blue due to the economic immobility factors mentioned above, but there is also another one that may be keeping a fair number of them together in their home states. It is the un-portability of unemployment benefits across state lines, as each state administers its own unemployment benefits. Many of the Blue states are crying the blues due to insolvency worries, dwindling tax bases, capital and commercial flight to Red states without so much as a fleeting question as to the causes of those trends like the individual states' treatment of their corporations and taxpayers.

The impoverished intransigent ideology

President Obama's famous statement about rural Americans was revealing, "It's not surprising then, they get bitter, clinging to guns or religion or antipathy to people who aren't like them or anti-immigrant sentiment or anti-trade sentiment as a way to explain their frustrations."

He may have been right about part of it.

When Americans feel abandoned they <u>do</u> close ranks and seek solace and comfort in that which gives them strength like their belief in God and their right to protect themselves. The vast majority of them do not appeal to their government (at least not yet) for a hand-out. The exception is the urban areas of some Blue states where poverty and food stamp levels are breaking all records.

141

Unfortunately, a convincing case can be made, that given the trends we're seeing in urban poor America, we will be forced to take some cities under receivership (like Detroit) and may witness, in the not too distant future, the creation of government-funded and dominated areas/zones that resemble bifurcated Cold War Germany.

No freedom-loving person wants that to happen, but it could unless tough measures are taken to rein in local government spending, re-negotiate extravagant municipal labor contracts (and pension contributions), offer more attractive municipal bonds based on sound forward-thinking market based economic reforms and relieve job-creating businesses of some of the restrictions that keep them from adding more jobs.

In short, incentives instead of penalties might breathe new life into some of the Blue states.

Rigid ideology that is based on economic theory and not practice, or that is not grounded in human nature, must give way to one that works. Soon, there will not be enough tax-generating companies or individuals in certain Blue states to pay for the running of their governments. Squeezing the balloon at one end forces the air to the other, and in human terms forces families to uproot themselves and move where the jobs and prosperity reside. These are the Red states.

There is one nagging question that begs an answer, "Will Democrats who leave Blue states for prosperous Red states bring their rigid ideology with them and try to transplant it in their new homes OR will they realize that by changing the economic dynamics of a successful Red state to a failing Blue state model they will effectively replicate the Blue state's problems and end up where they started?"

How Republicans can win in a changing America

The underlying question there really is, "Will committed Democrats see the light and vote Republican?" No one can really tell. All we can hope for is that their memories don't fade too much or too fast.

What will the future hold?

Will America also experience an increased hemorrhaging of people from its urban centers? Will suburbanites pull up stakes and look for quieter less expensive homes in near rural areas? Will a Democratic voter exodus from Blue states to Red states change the electoral balance in the Red states (and the same in their former Blue states) and create new opportunities for Democrats when re-districting time comes around again? Would it be a good thing for more states to turn Purple?

Republicans cannot and should not wait for the answers. They must realize that Blue state expats are potential change agents.

Their experiences and their reasons for moving present a very compelling narrative that can be used to convince other Democrats currently residing in Blue or Purple states that the big-government high-taxation Democratic Party model has failed and must be replaced.

Republicans would be wise to start gathering these personal stories now. They will need them, later.

Chapter 13

The changing voter marketplace:
Lesson plan for winning

The Republican Party organization: when not in Rome...

One quote from the American business world could apply to the current state of the Republican Party's organization, "They spent so much time getting re-organized that they never truly got organized!"

If you believe that, and the last two losing Presidential campaigns would seem to point in that direction, then what are the Republicans going to do to reverse the situation?

For half a millennium (or at least the last 300 years of its 500-year existence) the Roman Republic fought several civil wars to keep from unraveling, but unravel it did. It then saw the rise of Julius Caesar who was acclaimed, "Perpetual Dictator" in 44 B.C. five years after crossing the Rubicon River and effectively breaking the law of *Imperium* that required generals to disband their armies before proceeding south towards Rome.

We all know what happened to the Roman Republic (it was dissolved) and to Caesar (he was murdered) and later to Rome and the Italians (they became an economic basket case with national per capita debt of $43K, second only to the U.S.' $54K!).

The story of how the Roman Empire held on so long is a cautionary and instructive tale for Republicans who would like to regain power. The Romans knew the value of organization and education. They also knew that when both were combined with a large army that could exert enormous power they could extend their rule far beyond their own borders. At the Holy Roman Empire's zenith in 117 A.D., they controlled over one million square miles of territory that stretched from the tip of Britain to North Africa and east to modern day Iraq.

How Republicans can win in a changing America

The Romans were able to maintain their dominion through exceptional organization, forced loyalty and by adopting the methods of others when they were judged superior.

"It should be noted that the main reason for the Romans becoming masters of the world was that, having fought successively against all peoples, they always gave up their own practices as soon as they found better ones." (Charles-Louis de Montesquieu, 1689-1755). Unfortunately, the costs of maintaining such a large military as well as the growing corruption of its citizen soldiers and subsequent transference of their loyalty from the City of Rome to its generals led to the Empire's undoing (or so says Montesquieu).

What do the Roman Empire and the Republican Party have in common?

On the surface, we would have to say, 'not much' from an organizational point of view, especially when the comparison is made with the Empire at its heyday.

Looking at the Empire's decline, however, the comparisons are sobering. Today, Republicans don't control the principal levers of governmental power or set the political agenda. They don't have 'dominion' over a wide-ranging empire (the Senate or White House). Their generals (senior Republican leaders) are aging and many of their citizen soldiers (their base) are demoralized and depressed.

Their organization is badly in need of re-organization and the more vocal single-issue factions of the Party (along with some pretty disappointing candidates) are effectively preventing them from winning key battlefield victories as well as the hearts and minds of the more flexible members of the opposition.

In short, they have not managed to learn the lessons they need to turn defeat into victory. They are stuck in-between gears, suffering from a lack of purpose and direction.

Lesson #1: History repeats itself regardless of what men do

America has seen the political pendulum swing back and forth, often in direct correlation to the changes taking place in society, sometimes preceding it and sometimes following it. The party that accurately predicts the changes to come (not necessarily makes them happen) and prepares itself to take advantage of those changes will have a better chance of being ready for power when the election 'clock' strikes the hour.

For decades, the Republican Party counted on constancy - constancy of acceptance of its platform and doctrines often by a slim majority of voters. It changed only marginally along with the slow incremental societal change that didn't present an immediate threat to its relevance or alternative as America's ruling party.

A parallel can be drawn with the labor movement in Great Britain when the country's economic problems reached the doorstep of the common man and thus became the tipping point that finally led to the election of a conservative government formed under Prime Minister Margaret Thatcher.

Left-wing progressive labor union-dominated ideology bit the dust hard and for the first time in many years took a backseat to theory. It was, for Britain, not only the right time for change but the right change...just in time. America is getting perilously close to that point now, thanks to two back-to-back Democratic Party dominated administrations that have been characterized by a plethora of ideologically dangerous decisions that could well throw our country and maybe the entire planet into an economic tailspin from which it will take decades to recover.

What can Republicans do about history?

There is a movement by the left to re-write history and it includes the revisionist editing of schoolbook texts that would portray the USA as an oppressor, civil rights opponent and hegemonist power.

Revisionist history is alive and well on America's college campuses through committed left-leaning tenured professors who are installed for life in America's universities. In positions of authority, these people have free rein to concoct one-sided political dramas that serve their liberal agendas and present them as factual representations of American society for impressionable minds to consume...or else fail the course.

This stacked deck of daily historical 'spin' is also offered up on America's airwaves and the Internet by well-funded and committed liberal commentators and pundits who are in a state of perpetual overdrive, weaving a narrowly defined narrative that totally ignores the other side of the story.

A perfect example of this desire to upend history is the Obama camp's redefinition of what's *fair* and *balanced.* According to them and the Democratic Party faithful, these words have now come to mean what is *fair* to the administration and its policies for re-distributing America's wealth and power to *balance* the historical inequality created by greedy capitalists. If Americans didn't know better, we might think we are living in Cold War Soviet-dominated East Germany, so strong is the propaganda coming from the President and his Administration.

148

Make history - win elections

If the object of the game is to win elections, then the Rs must adopt a broad palette of tactics that <u>include but are not limited to</u> the *bold colors* that Ronald Reagan talked about in his 1975 speech to CPAC,

"Since our last meeting we have been through a disastrous election. It is easy for us to be discouraged, as pundits hail that election as a repudiation of our philosophy and even as a mandate of some kind or other. But the significance of the election was not registered by those who voted, but by those who stayed home.

If there was anything like a mandate it will be found among almost two-thirds of the citizens who refused to participate...our people look for a cause to believe in. Do we need a third party, or is it a new and revitalized second party, raising a banner of no pale pastels, but bold colors which make it unmistakably clear where we stand on all of the issues troubling the people?"

For many Republicans, Reagan's words have taken on almost biblical significance. While President Reagan was unquestionably a consummate politician, strategist and staunch defender of American values, we submit that to adopt his strategy of 1975 (the presentation of issues and the solutions <u>only in bold colors</u>) will fail at the ballot box in 2014 and 2016 unless seriously tweaked to show HOW the values of the Republican Party can turn around our current economic malaise.

America of 2013 is fragmented and distrustful of its authority figures, institutions and political leaders much more so than in 1980. While we thirst for truth, many of us are not sure we would recognize it if we saw it face-to-face, perhaps because we've been numbed by all the commercials, the cookie cutter

How Republicans can win in a changing America

town hall meetings and the photo ops with human backdrops and are simply fed up with the Madison Avenueing of our candidates.

American skepticism today is so pervasive that a straight-talker like Ronald Reagan would have a difficult time winning an election even WITH a billion dollars behind him!

Professor Eliot Cohen of Johns Hopkins University reinforced that same message in the March/April 2013 issue of the *Foreign Policy Magazine*, "...we do not live in Reagan's time, we do not face his challenges...the fact of the matter is that America is not quite what it was in 1980."

As a nation we're tired of being spun by the political class. We're fed up with subject shape-shifters who never answer our questions but instead use them as a bridge to nowhere topics. We're weary of incivility and character assassination by the media and by zealous politicians who seize every opportunity to play the race card, the gender card or the class card.

We'd like to come together, but we're worried and afraid that the process will somehow demean us, dilute our power or our views. We'd love to rally around a candidate who would actually KEEP a campaign promise, unlike the current occupant of the White House. We'd like to get off our duffs and vote, but we want to make sure that our votes count for something and are not just protests against the status quo.

Republicans have an opportunity to offer a nuanced, well thought out platform of policies that can take America forward along with smart candidates that know how to listen, react and act, but time's a wastin' and we had better get moving if we want to keep the House and gain seats in the Senate in 2014.

How Republicans can win in a changing America

Solution: Shore up the base with an optimistic and uplifting Reaganist message that is rooted in history and makes a clear *cause and effect connection* to <u>today</u> using recent historical comparisons that fit within the voter's generational frame of reference.

If history is going to repeat itself no matter what men decide to do, then let's focus on the positive historical accomplishments by Republicans and make a strong and undeniable connection to our Party (like the passage of the earlier Civil Rights legislation over the objections of the southern Democrats) and do it over and over again. History <u>will</u> repeat itself and America <u>will</u> return to its core beliefs and values. For Republicans it cannot come too soon.

Lesson #2: Bearding the lion in his den or how to counter lies, innuendo and insults from the Democrats

We live in a 24-hour news and entertainment cycle and as such we've become accustomed to seeing daily encounters between the Christians and the lions played out in living color on our HD flat screen TVs. In case anyone has the slightest doubt as to which is which, the Republicans are the ones who are unarmed and bear the scars of previous fangs and claws, courtesy of an obliging mainstream media that has opened the gates and let in the big cats.

<u>If Republicans are to start winning elections they must learn new ways of strategizing, communicating and interacting with Democrats in public fora.</u>

They must practice the art of *humor* and not retreat from poking fun at Democratic candidates or their surrogates. This goes double for encounters with the President, a man with a very thin skin and who has trouble with personal criticism.

151

Lampooning and satire have been an integral part of American culture and politics for centuries.

Republicans must learn to use humorous retorts on talk shows and in public settings to keep the opposition off balance.

Solution: Republicans must not shrink from a fight, but they must be careful that they are not regarded as too combative, as the left loves to paint them as shrill and *off-the-wall* (think their Tea Party characterizations). In short, we must fight but we must not let it look like a fight. Here's a hypothetical example...

Let's say that political polar opposites Chris Matthews and Sean Hannity are in the same room at the same table debating the same topic. Chris Matthews throws out the following, "Your party lost because you're morally bankrupt and your leaders are wimps and obstructionists." Instead of demurring from the argument, Hannity must meet force with equal and opposing force in a controlled and creative way using, among other tactics, pithy humor as the weapon of choice lest he be perceived to be weak (or shrill) and ineffectual (or unfeeling).

The more acerbic and belligerent the voice, the greater the need for humor and wit AND facts to turn that voice into one that reminds the viewer of a spoiled petulant child. Discipline is the key.

Using humor, Hannity responds, "Wow, Chris, I didn't realize you could actually string two sentences together without mentioning George Bush! I'm pleased to hear you're mellowing. I don't know how you can say that the Rs are morally bankrupt. Don't you first need to have an objective frame of reference to make those kinds of ridiculous charges?

How Republicans can win in a changing America

I think the Republicans have shown remarkable restraint by not burning you in effigy every time you flap your gums and throw out some ludicrous remark in broad daylight! Let's stick to the facts, man..." (a short fact or two that are 'soundbiteable' are then offered up by Mr. H). By doing all of this with a grin in a very relaxed manner that indicates he is not only composed and unshaken but also confident will move the audience' support his way.

There are situations where humor won't work, however, and it's up to the campaign managers to identify them and advise their clients, accordingly. No longer should Republicans be tempted to take the respectable high road and ignore the ignoramuses. If it is Chicago-style back alley brass knuckle politics that win the day and elections, then the Republicans must adapt. They must jump off the pedestal, roll up their sleeves, loosen their ties and choose tactics that work.

If the Democrats are going to sling mud, then Republicans better have a bigger shovel and know how to use it. Humor is still one of the many ways to disarm the opposition.

Lesson #3: Public speaking and how to stop the hecklers

Any Republican who accepts an invitation to speak publicly must be prepared to be skewered and heckled by the opposition or its surrogates, regardless of the venue. Democrats and Democrat-leaning special interest groups and NGOs (non-government organizations) are prepared to take the fight to the floor and will, if at all possible, hide their protest signs and other paraphernalia under their clothes and wait for the right moment to strike.

Solution(s): These days, nearly all venues have security, but it takes time for security to get to the hecklers and usher them out. There are several ways to handle them.

One is to start out your speech with a word about free speech like, "I value free speech like the rest of you, and I know that some of my remarks today might agitate some people. That's why I'd like to invite the hecklers among you to stand up now and be recognized.

Naturally, I'd prefer you to wait until the question and answer part of my speech, but I know that you want the media to see you so I'll understand if you want to be heard now. Just be aware that I'm a patient man. I just ask that you respect the audience who came to hear me not you."

This approach will earn you the respect of your audience and make it more difficult for the hecklers and/or protestors to get the audience on THEIR side later. If that doesn't work and you are still heckled, don't joust with them. Stand your ground. Take your speech from the podium and sit down beside it and look over your notes while security clears them from the room. Do not give the TV cameras the opportunity to capture your discomfort or displeasure at the podium.

No 'deer in the headlights' grimaces please. Be deliberate and poised in your actions and wait, patiently. Then, when things have calmed down, collect your notes, stand up and return to the podium and pick up where you left off. If it happens again, repeat the process. Resist the impulse to say anything belittling the protestors.

Instead, when you re-start your speech, you could say something like, "There's nothing like free speech...except maybe having the good sense to know *when* and *how* to use it."

The audience will be with you. The best public speaking is that which embraces the public's sense of fairness and makes them a stakeholder in your remarks. Try not to use a teleprompter, but you could have a teleprompter set up just so you can say, "Can someone please remove the teleprompter? I don't want anyone to confuse me with the President. I'd like to talk to you from the heart not from the screen."

Rehearse your speech carefully and if possible, write it yourself. That way you will be more comfortable with your own words. Know your audience before you even put pen to legal pad. In preparing your speech, insert a few local references that could create a personal bond between you and them.

Try to avoid the obvious sports references if possible as they are often seen as pandering. Instead, talk about a prominent Republican historical figure (preferably one who's not controversial but revered by the audience).

Take your time. Don't rush through the speech. Let each thought sink in. Make eye contact, left to right, front row to back row. Ask the people in the back if they can hear you. Speak in uplifted tones with enthusiasm and emotion.

DON'T mimic the *Obama staring off into the future with uplifted and out-jutted chin pose* unless you're angling for a spot on Mount Rushmore. Use hand gestures appropriately but sparingly.

When you are nearing the end of your talk, be sure to speed up a little and lift your voice up a notch. End on a high note of optimism. It's best to be remembered for your passion and commitment, and don't forget to thank everybody, again, for the invitation to speak.

If your speech is to be made available to the media, make sure that they get it either shortly before its delivery or embargo it until delivery. Don't deviate too much from your prepared remarks so that the media feels confident they can quote you from the speech text.

The Q and A

The question and answer period is a time to clarify and expand your thoughts. Sometimes it's for redemption (if the speech has not been terribly well-received). It's also the time for *asking for the sale* and issuing another call to action if they missed the first.

Listen carefully to the questions. If the questioners have not given their names, ask them who they are and then address them by name. If sound levels in the hall are low or if the question is barely audible, repeat the question so the rest of the audience and the media hear it by saying, "Just so I understand, you asked..." Then answer it succinctly without segueing or spinning it into another topic (audiences are weary of that particular political tactic). Ask the questioner if that satisfied them. If they say, 'no,' smile politely and suggest that they give their name to your staff and, in the interest of time - and to get to as many questions as possible, someone will get back to them with a more detailed response.

The denouement: Tying up the loose ends

At the end of the Q&A period thank everybody for being there, thank the host, smile and raise your hand in a farewell gesture and leave the stage after you take a moment to savor the applause. Remember that the media is present and may be filming this so don't leave prematurely. Finally, make sure that you shake hands with everyone on the stage.

Lesson #4: Tie them up in court or in committee hearings

Most Americans would agree that we have a legal system that is in dire need of reform. There are probably very few of us, however, who would hire a lawyer that refused to use every aspect of the system to win our case. If that's true, we certainly shouldn't feel pangs of conscience in holding our opponents accountable for their actions in a Congressional Committee, a court of law or the court of public opinion.

To ignore their use in furthering our search for the truth (Benghazi, Fast and Furious, the IRS and NSA scandals, to name a few) would not only be a grave tactical error but also an inexcusable sin of commission when those avenues are at our disposal. It is one sin Republicans can ill afford to commit on the way to 2014 and beyond.

The Benghazi hearings are a perfect example of what we believe is a Constitutionally-defensible attempt to assign responsibility for actions (or inactions) of members of the Executive Branch and others that could be linked to the death of four Americans, the destruction of our Consulate and CIA annex in Libya and the lies surrounding the CAUSE of the attacks.

Republicans must be steadfast in their search for the truth even if it reveals their own errors in judgment or wrongdoing in their own party. Anything less would give the opposition ample justification to label the hearings as 'partisan.' *(They will anyway, but it's best not to give them the hook to hang that hat on.)*

Keeping up the pressure is important to the Republicans' success, but they must avoid the appearance of being unfair when applying it.

When questioning witnesses, Committee members must be direct but respectful and above all <u>not make speeches instead of asking questions.</u> They should probe but with probity because the camera is unforgiving and so are the mainstream media, Op Ed writers and bloggers not to mention the Democrat spin machine.

Lesson #5: Broadening the political base is the only way to win

The election of 2012 showed that Republicans directed their messages to a very narrow base of voters and suffered mightily for it. Not only did they not get enough of their own base to turn out, but they also largely ignored three very important voter demographic groups: young women, Hispanics and Black voters. *(See Chapter 15 for strategies for winning.)*

Had three million voters from these groups voted Republican, Mitt Romney would have won by 52% instead of Barack Obama. It is highly doubtful that solid Blue states like California, New York, Massachusetts, Minnesota and Illinois and others will turn Red overnight, but it is possible for the Republicans to turn a few of them Purple over time with an improved organization, highly targeted voter group messaging and by a full court press on the ground. In Chapter 4 we discussed the various types of voters Republicans must court next time around, but winning over these voters will fail if the Rs use the same message on them that was directed to solid Red state voters in 2012.

Solution: The message and the issues must be re-framed in order to win. Republicans will need to appeal to those three million Democrat and independent voters in a new and compelling way, on their turf, using *their* language.

This is not to say they that the Rs will need to make a wholesale change in their political ideology; but they will need to fine tune

How Republicans can win in a changing America

their messaging and step up their efforts for getting out the vote (as well as re-thinking and possibly modifying their platform/policies somewhat to appeal to these new, potential Republican supporters).

Republicans must use the media more effectively and that goes for the social media as well.

The importance of having a well thought out social media strategy along with professionally-crafted messages that regularly hit their youthful targets is one of the most obvious takeaways of the last election. Democrats dominated the narrative among younger voters through their presence on 'Twitter' and in 'Facebook.' Republicans must begin setting up small special interest discussion groups within the Party and throughout the country that look at the issues that drive single interest and special interest voters, and they must host these discussions in these voters' physical locations and through webcasting.

Before all this happens there must be national dialogue on what it means to be a Republican and whether or not the Party can accommodate some of the opposition's views and maybe meet them half-way with policies that do not radically conflict with core Republican beliefs and values.

After achieving a consensus within the Party on the big issues that drive the vote within the three voter groups mentioned, the Party leadership must craft sound, workable and compelling arguments that can be used to persuade them to think about voting Republican. It goes without saying that Republicans must devise a better strategy for approaching minority voters in the United States to convince them that the Rs are not an elitist party but one that has the hopes and aspirations of their minority communities at heart.

A constant reminder of the southern Democrats' earlier opposition to passage of Civil Rights Legislation (along with other examples) must take center stage. This is not pandering. It is honest politics! We must begin to see voter groups for what they are – small, but important microcosms of subcultures with single issue interests.

Many of these voters do not vote based on a thorough review and analysis of the issues. They vote on the basis of their own personal situation and out of emotion. If Republicans are to garner a solid percentage of these votes, they must <u>earn</u> them by making a combined emotional and logical appeal while avoiding the traditional Republican approach of fighting opposing viewpoints with facts alone.

Birthing new Republicans

"It's elementary (school) my dear Watson." You don't have to be Sherlock Holmes to know that the education of a well-informed electorate starts in early childhood. Republicans' success is directly dependent upon having objective, honest educational materials that portray American history accurately - without political bias - so that decisions taken in the historical period in question are viewed in their own context and not linked to some overarching 'right wing conspiracy to oppress the middle class throughout the ages.' These historical events and decisions must be discussed free from modern-day judgmentalism or ideological influence, <u>by teachers who don't bring their biases into the classroom.</u>

If Republicans are to protect future voters from becoming victims of historical revisionism, then they must insist on having a seat at the editing table before the textbooks are printed.

160

In states like Texas that buy over five million textbooks for their public school pupils it's important to have a seat at that table.

(Critics frequently say that Texas forces its ideological views on the rest of the states/customers simply because publishers want the big Texas order and will accommodate revisions more easily than they would from a smaller customer.)

True, the Texas State Board of Education does have power, but it also has a broad mandate. It approves curriculum standards, textbooks and supplemental materials for all of its public schools. In that regard, it's not that different from other states, except that its reach is geographically bigger with more 'clients' to serve. The detractors don't seem to realize or care that the Board has fifteen members from fifteen very large districts and that they are selected in open elections, helping to ensure that the views of the communities are represented.

Granted, there could be more members and a larger Board, but consensus is difficult enough to reach with fifteen members let alone one for every few thousand people in a state the size of Texas. At some point, a state must set a limit if it is to accomplish anything on time.

Every selection committee or school board that must review, accept and order teaching materials will find itself at the center of controversy at some point or another unless it represents a state or jurisdiction that has a nearly 100% homogeneous viewpoint. Get ready for the inevitable disagreements and conflicts that are part of the process. Prepare for them and you won't be caught off-guard.

Vigilant not vigilante

In order to break the back of entrenched progressive teaching and historical revisionism in our schools, Republicans must be vigilant about learning the workings of their states' school board textbook selection process and they must stand for election to their local school boards. There is no other viable alternative, certainly not the extreme example of the educational vigilante who dons a white robe and burns the books he doesn't like.

Choose your books carefully and choose your teachers *extremely* carefully. We may not be able to completely weed out the ultra-partisan teacher from our schools, but there is something we <u>can</u> do to keep those biased teachers in check. We must demand that a fair and balanced curriculum be taught to our primary school-age children, because if it's not, we will be behind the curve when the next real test comes.

That test will come in high school and later, in college, where the impressionable minds of our teenagers are exposed to a potent cocktail...the powerful influence of educators only a decade or two older than themselves who are all too willing to parrot the biases of the mainstream media and pop-culture *news* shows.

The teenage years are years of high activity levels and often extraordinary temptation. High schoolers are often dismissive of their parents, their teachers and their government, none of which they really understand. American Civics or American Government studies have nearly gone the way of the Dodo Bird. Students today couldn't tell you how a bill is passed or a cabinet is formed or why there are thirteen stripes and fifty stars on Old Glory.

How Republicans can win in a changing America

It's our own fault. We haven't challenged them or told them why it's important.

If Republicans are not ready to cede either the moral high ground or the education breeding ground to liberal or Progressive thought then they must work with local school boards and school administrators to improve the teaching of government and *governance* and make it RELEVANT to the lives of high school students.

Young Republican groups must also be formed and run in much the same way as that bastion of youthful entrepreneurism, *Junior Achievement*, has been run for nearly one hundred years.

The science, art and practice of politics must become a living, breathing thing. It must be shown for not only what it is but more importantly for what it can become when smart, dedicated, young people understand the principles of conservatism and know how to apply those principles in their daily lives to *change* their daily lives!

In fact, there might be some value in merging the study of entrepreneurism with the young Republican group. By providing important career-path guidance along with an ideological blueprint for achieving students' goals, Republicans will gain an advantage with these new voters and assure a fair comparison with the views of liberal big government advocates.

These groups must be led by dynamic individuals from the local community who understand the importance of their mission. They must encourage critical thought among their youthful members AND show the clear cause and effect nexus using modern-day examples. (It will do no good to dwell on those from a century ago.)

Finally, political youth groups must join forces with the high school debating society in order to sharpen their members' public speaking skills so they can present their thoughts to a wider audience. The media can and should be an important ally in the entire process as well. Republicans must court the media and make it aware that they are not indoctrinating America's teens; they are engaging and challenging them to think on their feet and to stand on their own and eventually evolve into high information voters.

The last and most difficult group to court is the college student. While most large campuses have young Democrat and young Republican organizations, they are usually populated by those who've already made up their minds about which ideology they prefer.

If Republicans are to glean more potential voters from the college student population they must work for them and realize two things: 1. conservatism has never been the dominant political force on America's campuses and 2. the cards are stacked against Republicans because of liberal-leaning professors and the natural urge among college students to rebel against the status quo which most view as controlled by *the moneyed power brokers of Wall Street in collusion with their Republican cronies on the Hill.*

Either way, it's a steep hill to climb, but climb it Republicans must if they are ever going to win elections when the opposition Democrat candidate speaks with a youthful tongue and has an even more youthful appearance. Achieving Republican victories in the college environment will rely on role modeling and bringing charismatic, respected leaders from the Republican ranks of the business, cultural and civic communities onto campus. Success sells.

College students just need to know that Republicans stand for CHOICES and that by choosing the conservative Republican path they will have <u>more choices and more opportunities</u> in the marketplace, and in society at large. This is, admittedly, a tough sell, because most college-age young people probably don't associate choice with Republicans.

They associate Republicanism with their parents (even if they weren't party members) who were always telling them what they <u>couldn't do</u> rather than suggesting good alternatives: don't have premarital sex, don't get an abortion, don't take drugs, don't drink and drive, don't stay out late, don't smoke and don't hang around in bad company.

Who could blame them for turning liberal? The free, liberal and sometimes libertine path is exciting. The conservative path is not (or at least that's the way it's been portrayed). This attitude has to change, but it won't change overnight. It will only happen when conservatism and the Republicans become viable alternatives.

As previously mentioned, we must find role models who identify with the various ethnic groups we're trying to befriend and who have a success story to tell. One sterling example is Dr. Ben Carson, a Black neurosurgeon who spoke eloquently about the hazards of economic excess and Obamacare at the National Prayer breakfast in 2013 and later at CPAC.

The great Republican makeover

Republicans should not be laboring under the misconception that they will ever be seen as *cool* to the cool crowd. They should aim, instead, to be viewed as *acceptable* or *non-threatening*.

That means that the pop culture media (the Daily Show with Jon Stewart, the Colbert Report, David Letterman Show, etc.) must begin to tone down their attacks on Republicans.

In order for them to do that, they will have to be convinced that the Republicans have a sense of humor.

Other comedians who already indulge in *homespun* humor must do more self-effacing Republican jokes AND start pinging Democrats in a pointed but good natured way so as to show the pop culture media, college students and the vast number of twenty-somethings out there that Republicans have that sense of humor. Again, offer the choice and make the choice attractive. When you have them by their funny bone, their hearts and minds will, inevitably, follow.

Teaching the dog to hunt: Twenty new tactics for Republican candidates

Every West Point graduate has studied famous battles of the past - from both sides of the battlefield. This includes the commanders in the field, their strategies and especially their tactics. Nothing is overlooked. From the unique perspective of hindsight, cadets can recreate history and apply new alternative battle plans and then through computer modeling predict the outcomes and the winners.

If Republicans are to gain more ground, win fresh converts to their ideology and new votes for their party and candidates, they must adopt some new tactics because, quite frankly, the old ones aren't working well enough.

Here are 20 specific suggestions for newly-minted Republican candidates to consider:

1. If you feel you can't answer the question you're asked by the media, say, "I'm not sure I can give you a definitive answer, but let me have a go at it." Then, re-frame it if necessary and answer your own way. By doing so you will come off as honest and thoughtful and not an 'evader' of the truth.

2. Avoid giving your own personal opinion on hot-button, potentially incendiary social issues. Instead, say that, "America is a melting pot of ideas and lifestyles. I trust Americans to solve many of our problems, together. What I believe is not as important as what you believe and want me to advocate for once I'm elected. Not everything can or should be legislated, especially at the Federal level." Saying this will earn you high marks as one who will listen to his constituency.

3. Never send out emails that incorporate humor or irony, and never send any emails to women that contain personal remarks or ambiguities. A good rule of thumb is to copy someone else on the cc line for corroboration, later, in case you need it. Remember, the long knives of the opposition have no scabbards and are always out.

4. Never let a personal attack go un-countered. Respond quickly and decisively but calmly. Americans have a sixth sense about unfair attacks and generally side with the victim (recipient of the attack). Because of that you will probably not need to say much. Just make sure to act genuinely taken aback.

5. Use 'dismissive humor' when talking about the opposition's roughhouse, Chicago-style tactics. "You know what they're like, always trying to pick a fight. Maybe they'll wise up, someday and realize that Americans want their elected officials to act like grown-ups and not schoolyard bullies." Sucker-punching is sucker-punching. In some environments, it's acceptable, but if

167

you're trying to maintain a level of seriousness and professionalism, call out the tactic and denounce it.

6. Never let an opponent filibuster an answer. If you need to, interrupt them and say something like, "My honorable opponent must be paid by the word. This is what's wrong with our government, too much loose and empty rhetoric." THIS will connect you to the common man because nobody likes a blowhard.

7. Don't be lured into commenting on subjects where your knowledge is thin. This is a typical interviewer's trick. Ask for a different question by saying, "Now that's an interesting question, if only I had an interesting answer for you. The truth is I'm not an expert on that, but I have advisors who are and I can probably get you the answer by tomorrow. In the meantime, how about a different question?"

8. Don't be 'out-facted.' Instead, say, "Facts are curious things, especially these days, when everybody seems to have his own. I don't believe the American people need constant instant-replays of facts or a lecture to know that something is very wrong. We may not all have the same level of understanding of the issue, but we are all able to recognize a problem when we see it."

9. When heckled, ask the heckler to submit his question in writing to your staff. Say, "The First Amendment only guarantees free speech. Unfortunately, it doesn't make you smart enough to know when and where to use it."

10. Always have another person in the room when a young woman meets with you or, at the very least, keep your door open. Never meet a female staffer or co-worker alone, especially after hours.

How Republicans can win in a changing America

11. Whenever possible don't refer to ethnic groups with hyphens. Instead say, "fellow Americans."

12. Don't drive an expensive car to meetings or to rallies. Don't be photographed at expensive restaurants, on yachts, in private planes or shopping at exclusive stores. Nobody wants to be reminded of your wealth or privilege.

13. Feign interest even when there's none. Don't look bored or confused. Look INTERESTED.

14. Take notes, even if there are none to take. Who knows? A good idea might come to you while you're doing it.

15. Loosen or take off your tie and relax at a town hall meeting if the audience appears responsive to such a move and sit on the same level as the audience.

16. Vet and double-vet your staff (by objective third parties). Talk to them yourself to get a feel for their poise and knowledge. Then get them to sign a legally-binding no-tell pledge before they start working for you.

17. Hire professionals - not political zealots or 'yes men' to do your opposition research.

18. Do not appear on politically one-sided television shows where the host has a record of personal assassination politics. If you can't avoid it, however, <u>prepare well</u>, look attentive and smile a lot at the right places AND DON'T TAKE THE BAIT of leading cul-de-sac questions. Remember, though you're doing damage control on such shows, you still have an opportunity to change a few minds and maybe some votes.

19. Always come across as one of the common men and be seen doing ordinary things (only if you can do them well).

20. Never speak ill of another Republican.

Dealing with scandals 101

The Obama Administration hit the trifecta in May 2013 with three massive scandals that knocked it off its axis and put it squarely on the defensive. Congressional investigative committees smelled blood in the water and went into high gear. Though there were no bets wagered, even the casual observer could have predicted that an administration that couldn't keep its ducks in a row would end up defending an indefensible lack of management of the machinery of government.

Getting grilled on Benghazi-gate, the AP surveillance scandal and the IRS targeting of conservative groups (and later the NSA snooping scandal), the Obama Administration learned all too well that what can go wrong will go wrong as the über nasty atmosphere on Capitol Hill has proved. For the Republicans, there are many lessons to be learned from this experience, some of which can be applied to dealing with scandals in general.

Let's take a look at the investigative committee hearings on Benghazi to see how they conducted themselves and what might be learned, in hindsight, from the experience.

Congressional hearings offer something for everybody: salacious media sound bites, damning testimony, grandstanding, face time for Congressional Representatives and sometimes redemption for the accused. Knowing all that's riding on hearings and the damage that can be done to the reputations of companies, government agencies and individuals, it's surprising how poorly both the interrogators and the interrogated perform when the house lights go on! As far as Congressional Committee Representatives go, they are blessed with (and sometimes cursed by) staffers who gather information, do research and prep them before the mikes go live.

When the Chairman hits the gavel calling the meeting to order and the cameras start whirring, the mood always becomes tense. Republicans and Democrats go to their respective corners, and come out swinging when the bell sounds.

Within the first few minutes it becomes abundantly clear to the audience without even seeing a name or party designation on a tent card which representative will go on the attack and which one will defend. It usually breaks along party lines but not always with equal ferocity. The group dynamic of the Benghazi hearings was a perfect case in point. While the Republicans aggressively interrogated each and every witness, they didn't all use the same tactics.

Theirs was a curious combination of bad cop interrogation and the not-so-friendly country lawyer approach used by the late Senator Sam Ervin of North Carolina when he participated in the McCarthy and Watergate hearings. Some gave long opening statements (specifically targeted for the record) and others sought the *afterlife repetitiousness* of the media with short, dramatically delivered questions designed to be played and replayed for wider audiences on TV and the Internet.

The latter represent the new young lions of the party who used the hearings to burnish their party credentials with their colleagues and the folks back home. Procedure dictates that the Chair moves from majority to minority party member. Each revealed from the outset the tone their party decided to adopt: from attacker to defender or from predator to protector.

171

The Benghazi hearings were steeped with emotion and intrigue as were the IRS hearings. Both shared one thing: an effort to uncover in detail the astounding breach of confidence that the government created through its actions.

In Benghazi, the players were the top decision-makers of the federal government, the CIA, DOD and STATE, and none were terribly interested in being put on the Congressional hot seat. One of those was then Secretary of State, Hillary Clinton, who definitely lost her cool.

Exasperated after being questioned by a Republican committee member she curtly stated, "With all due respect, the fact is we had four dead Americans. Was it because of a protest or was it because of guys out for a walk one night decided to go kill some Americans? What difference at this point does it make?"

Republicans should all thank Mrs. Clinton for these remarks; they are a valuable lesson which is: *always maintain your composure especially when you're being videotaped for posterity.* Under normal circumstances, Republicans have a strong kinship with, or at least understanding of, the CIA and the military and would probably have been willing to moderate their questioning, but Benghazi was different and everyone knew it. These hearings weren't looking at a philandering President or a real estate transaction gone awry.

The subject was the abuse of power and the death of four Americans...and a cover-up of the real reasons behind the attack on our Consulate and annex in Libya. On balance, Republicans acquitted themselves well apart from a few thespian-like utterances. They maintained their composure and left their diatribes in the drawer.

How Republicans can win in a changing America

Seeing that, the Democrats were forced to retrieve the *partisan card* from their vest pocket and play it shamelessly, accusing the Republicans of grandstanding and using the seriousness and sanctity of the hearing environment for their own political purposes.

As more facts about the twelve iterations of the Benghazi talking points and the video-blaming came out, the White House became more and more defensive to the point where the President added more fuel to the fire by calling the hearings a "*sideshow*."

This was a tactical error and a very poor choice of words that most Americans would find repugnant even if they were supporters of the President. To the Republicans' credit, they stayed on message and redoubled their efforts to peel back the onion and seek the truth about Benghazi, and though the Administration (and the mainstream media) had actively downplayed the scandal for months, the public's attention span was still reasonably fresh.

This enabled the Republicans to maintain their appearance as truth-seekers and helped them to deflect the Administration's attempts to paint them as bald-faced partisans on a "witch hunt" (an epithet used by White House spokesman Jay Carney to describe the hearings). Scandals are part and parcel of American political life. Every administration must expect them AND have a plan to deal with them. That goes for their political parties, too.

The fallout from scandals can often taint political parties for many years and adversely affect future candidates' chances for election. While the odd individual scandal can sometimes end with an administration's term, it is not, however, deleted from the hard drive of the collective American consciousness.

How Republicans can win in a changing America

Republicans take heed. If history is any guide, your turn will come and you will end up on the other side of the table. Do yourselves a favor and have a plan and stick to it.

The impending Hillary Tsunami - Knowing thine opposition

You don't have to be an oceanographer to know that in 2013/14 America will experience a Hillary Clinton tsunami of massive never-ending waves of media coverage. Why? She could be the first female President of the United States (she's already a powerful and popular woman among the Democratic base voters, a consummate political animal AND a survivor).

Her four years spent in the Obama Administration was really about checking an important box - the political equivalent of doing community service for a competitor she forcefully opposed in 2008. It was the traditional *kiss and make up* or *bury the hatchet* that almost always accompanies a marginal political loss, especially within the Democratic Party.

We must give her credit. She did it well, apart from the Benghazi scandal where Americans lost their lives due to her alleged indecision. This has shown that the luster of her diamond tiara is only the reflected glow of the Clinton name and the distant memory of better times. Ironically, though, to Hillary Clinton and many Democrats, <u>that is enough</u>.

Memories, especially grossly embellished ones, are the genetic underpinnings of legends which, when given the right marketing and time, turn ordinary people into heroes and heroines who can, with enough hype, morph into leaders. What they will do AS leaders is another question. The year 2014 will see a massive *draft Hillary* movement as her former supporters who were reluctant acolytes for Barack Obama begin to come home.

How Republicans can win in a changing America

It won't take much to re-ignite the Hillary for President flame because it never went completely out! She saw to that with four years spent traveling the world burnishing her international foreign policy credentials as Secretary of State. The result: one profile sufficiently raised in a strangely apolitical way. She positioned herself perfectly as a candidate who is comfortable and knowledgeable with domestic policy, foreign policy and legislative affairs.

Given the rise of American secularism and the deification of the low-information and female voter, Hillary's time has come...unless she is unmasked and viewed as many see her: an ultra-liberal, highly impatient, chronically intolerant, extraordinarily calculating and sometimes vengeful person. *Benghazi-gate* may be that loose thread that ultimately unravels her political facade, enabling people to see the 'emperor' without any clothes. Time and events will tell.

For the Republicans, Hillary Clinton is the ultimate lesson in politics. Who would have thought that after such a dismal performance as the *First Lady of Healthcare* during her husband's Presidency, coupled with her role in *Travelgate* and the *Whitewater Scandal* along with her stubborn support for a philandering man who rubbed her nose in <u>his</u> dirty laundry, she would rise so fast and come so far? While there is such a thing as *luck* in politics, it can never replace shrewdness, flexibility and an elephantine skin. Americans like winners almost as much as they like victims, and Hillary Clinton has been both.

People can identify with her and more importantly, FORGIVE her missteps because they view her as slightly flawed (like themselves), but a fighter, capable of getting up off the mat after receiving a terrible beating. It's no coincidence that the sport of boxing is a powerful metaphor for life, especially political life, because it literally exudes Americanism.

175

It has its underdogs, *comeback kids*, and the aging but determined veteran who fights the younger more powerful titleholder. Boxing is every man and every woman.

Boxing Hillary

Hillary came into the ring a novice, got knocked down, lost by a TKO, got some great coaching and a makeover, found the eye of the tiger and re-entered the squared circle. It's her home turf and that of many Democrat office-holders and candidates who see themselves as folk heroes and standard-bearers for their ideology. This is a dilemma or certainly a challenge for Republicans. How do you fight mythology AND a willing audience that laps it up like an afternoon soap opera?

It's one thing to know your opponent well, and most political strategists know Hillary well. It's quite another thing to be able to counterpunch with her. After eight years of Obama, even the Democrats will be tired and will want a fresh campaign and a new standard-bearer. Hillary's the one! Her tsunami will hit America's shores in many waves and take many forms. A simple look back at her post-college pre-Bill Clinton life and her 2008 Presidential campaign should give the uninitiated a hint at how Hillary will re-construct and re-package herself for sale to her 'new village' of supporters for 2016.

One of the big differences, we predict, will be an intensified institutional "It takes a village" approach to consensus-making. She will build her momentum and move her message of *American reunification* through multiplier organizations rallying women (especially young college women), minorities (the Hispanic community, primarily), the homosexual community, senior women (the sisterhood) and disaffected Republicans (especially moderate Republican women) to the Democrat cause.

176

<u>One lingering question remains (just as it did with Ronald Reagan), "Will Hillary be too old (nearly 70) to withstand the rigors of the world's most challenging job?"</u>

Who knows? One thing is for certain, her style will be anything but shrill, and she will aspire to be her Party's equivalent to Ronald Reagan – paternalistic, trustworthy with a twist of new ageism, an American healer. During her husband's first term, we heard from Hillary herself that she was no 'Betty Crocker,' now we will hear from her surrogates that she's got gravitas in domestic and foreign policy matters and can punch as a heavyweight.

Critics will warn that, if elected, hers will be a *Tupperware-like* Presidency. Instead of pursuing a *one size fits all* agenda and solution-making like Barack Obama (think Obamacare), hers will be a populist *many sizes fit all* one where America's issues get separated and debated by special commissions and groups that are stacked with Democrats and get *burped* (vetted) in town hall meetings and public fora. After that, the next step will be sending the 'peoples' recommendations to the Congress bearing the *Good Public's Seal of Approval*, accompanied by a big "I dare you" to vote them down.

Hillary's supporters and potential voters include the rich, powerful and connected (and those who want to be), Baby Boomers, women's organizations, minorities, the poor, the unemployed, and literally anybody who's ever had a mother or a sister. Her biggest asset is her live-in banker, mentor and sometime sparring partner, the 42nd President of the United States. Bill Clinton's foundation, his contacts, contributors, venues and microphone are all Hillary's for the asking, and use them she will.

She will enjoy the chivalrous deference of *traditional* men because she's a woman (that is as long as she doesn't have any more Benghazi hearing-type outbursts). Her coat of gender protection will keep her warm if she plays her cards right.

The media's affection and support for Barack Obama, which is due in large part to his smashing the color barrier, will be seamlessly transferred to the woman who will break the nation's next societal barrier, that of the first female President.

There is a lot riding on 2016. The Democrats see Hillary's election as the next logical step to not only break through the ultimate glass ceiling, but to be the second position *runner* on the Presidential relay race team who will hand off the baton to the next Democratic (presumably minority) candidate in 2024 to complete the circle of racial and gender 'equality.'

The Republicans need to get off the starting blocks early if they're going to compete in THIS race.

Hillary Clinton is beatable

Republicans must realize that there is an ocean of voters who crave style over substance AND who will choose the charismatic bantam-weight fighter over the heavyweight businessman cum governor (like Romney) any time. In the America of 2012, likeability trumped capability and will probably continue for years to come.

If Republicans truly want to win in 2016, they must acknowledge the new reality of the changing voter 'marketplace' that includes style over substance voters and watch how the opposition courts them.

How Republicans can win in a changing America

They must learn from their mistakes and use their opponents' history against them. In Hillary's case, there are many mile markers in her past that blow her political cover:

1. her core left-wing ideology from her early post-college years

2. her failure to 'play well with others' in her ingénue role as healthcare czar in her husband's first term and

3. her bungled leadership of the State Department and its 'out-to-lunch' performance in the Benghazi affair

Republicans must not let the American electorate be sold a Pinto masquerading as a Mazerati. This is true whether the candidate is Mrs. Clinton or any other Democrat ideologue.

The Rs must suit up, hit the training camps, watch the instant replays, coach their protégé candidates better, harden them for 15 rounds but encourage them to go for the knockout when they see an opening. Politics is messy, but so is life. The difference is that one of them gives you a chance for a rematch.

Chapter 14

Cultivating change:
Growing new candidates

T he question of our modern age must be...

"Why would anyone want to go into politics considering the low esteem the public has for public office-holders?"

Like the mountain climber, who when asked why he climbs the highest peaks answers "because they're there," candidates often have simple straightforward public responses like, "to serve my country, to make a difference for my children, to protect America's ideals and values," etc.

Before we start administering political DNA testing, Meyers-Briggs and a lie detector to all who would run for office, we should start by re-phrasing the question, substituting the words *public service* for *politics* and repeat them often. Somehow the term just seems to fit better with the altruism that lies at the core of why serious people with serious motives are willing to lie down on the path to political office and let their opponents (and even some of their fellow party members and supporters) run over them!

Why would anyone who is already successful in their chosen profession gladly open up themselves, their family and friends, past successes and every word they ever uttered or wrote to scrutiny and possible public ridicule or vilification? The answer is still honor, duty, love of country and the desire to make a difference. No candidate is totally immune from the criticism of his peers, his opponents or the media, but some are given a 'pass.' Usually those candidates only representing liberal or Progressive thought get such a pass because that is the ideology the majority of the media holds dear (read: it's human to err and we must always forgive our side, but not our opponents because they are always wrong).

How Republicans can win in a changing America

So, the real question then becomes, "Why would anyone want to throw his hat into the ring as a REPUBLICAN candidate?"

A cynic or dyed in the wool liberal or Progressive will tell you it's because Republicans want to protect the status quo and maintain the unfair and unfettered dominance over the economy by the fat cat capitalists and to insure the hegemony of Wall Street bankers over the common man.

He will also say that it's because Republicans don't believe in true equality for women or minorities; because they want prayer and religion back in the schools and in the public square. Furthermore, it's because they support war as a means of conflict resolution and preemptive military strikes on foreign countries; because they believe everybody should be carrying a gun and they don't care about protecting children AND because they're just, well, greedy and egotistical.

If that were the truth, NOBODY would vote for ANY candidate espousing such views! But that's not the truth, and every Republican knows it. The trouble is that not enough moderate Democrats and Independents know it, and that has to change.

Enter the new Republican candidate

He's an unashamed protector of the Constitution, a supporter of the nuclear family, believes in personal responsibility and accountability, community service and civil discourse. He obeys the laws of the land, loves his country, family and friends, is formally educated AND streetwise and can speak passionately to a large audience and not AT them with a teleprompter. He believes in compromise on the details but fidelity to larger truths and ideals. He values America's diversity but is not afraid to criticize certain special interest groups or organizations when necessary.

182

He's not afraid to mix it up with the opposition but does so without raising his voice or resorting to personal attacks. He believes in shared responsibility and a level playing field, offering equal opportunity, but stops short of forced redistribution of wealth or awarding the *victim* label to whole groups of people.

He's for fair and consistent application of the law and doesn't regard America's laws as mere guidelines for relativist decision-making. He honors the rights of all people, not just those of the group du jour. He stands with the downtrodden and those down on their luck, believing that America owes its citizens a *targeted* shot at the American dream.

He supports access to the institutions of learning that will prepare them for the attempt. He believes in legitimizing (not offering amnesty or immediate citizenship) the status of America's illegal immigrants but not without extracting a promise from them to abide by our laws and to join the ranks of a multi-ethnic society by learning our language and our ways. He's passionate about his religion, but accepts and respects other faiths or people holding none. He's patriotic about America, but critical of her when necessary.

He admires and respects our military and values their service to our country and would never give them an order that was politically-motivated.

We had such a candidate in 2012 and his name was Willard (Mitt) Romney, but he fell a few million votes short of winning, not because he lacked ability but because America had changed since 2008 and because the Democrats better understood that change and how to capitalize on it!

In four short years, America's cynicism level went from dangerously high to toxic. The existing polarization of voter, ethnic, class and gender groups was exacerbated by the use of a deliberate strategy of *divide and conquer* by a President and his party that drowned out the tiny voices of truth and reason that could counter the unfair labels and attitudes ascribed to Republicans. Candidate Romney wasn't the only one that lost. The conservative movement lost, too. The Democrats did their job well.

Not only did they vanquish a candidate and marginalize a party, but they also temporarily killed off hope among 48% of voting Americans (and with those Republicans who stayed home). For the short term, they tarred future Republican candidates with the same brush of innuendo and lies about Republicans' motives that they used on Mitt Romney.

Americans are by nature optimists, but optimism alone will not help Republicans grow new candidates for national office. Much must be done in the years ahead to locate, vet and nurture candidates that can WIN over voter cynicism and the chicanery practiced by the opposition.

This is a long-term process, and the candidates with long-term potential are **not** necessarily the ones Republicans should be running in 2014 if they expect to win.

In addition to competent incumbents, the Party must choose from a pool of state office-holders and even political outsiders who have demonstrated coolness under fire, true leadership, sound decision-making AND who measure up to the ideological requirements listed above. These likely candidates must be vetted thoroughly.

Not a single one of them can be allowed to slip through the cracks and end up as the Republicans' choice, only to embarrass them in the home stretch of a campaign by scandal or foolish statements that de-legitimize their candidacy.

Republican precincts all throughout the USA have a bounty of potential candidates for national office in their midst. They know their strengths and their weaknesses well, and because they do, it is their responsibility to choose the best and introduce them to party officials who can help mold and shape their future candidacies. By providing them with small speaking venues, they can test the potential candidates' capabilities and their communication skills and put the best of them on a path towards larger venues and more substantive challenges.

The campaign lines for the Congressional and Senate elections of 2014 are already drawn. Most of the candidates have already been identified and the next part of the process (the primaries) will be put under the microscope of the media, especially those who wish to see Republican candidates fail.

That's why each primary challenger must remember that every single thing he says is possible fuel for the Democrats' bonfire. Early roasting of local Republican candidates provides good sound bites and fertile fodder for seasoned Democrat state committees to pass up the line to the smear merchants in ambush PACS like Organizing for America, etc. Caution must be the watchword for 2014's Republican candidates lest the Party LOSE seats rather than gain them.

A reminder: in 2014 all 435 House seats are up for grabs along with 33 Senate seats.

The outcome of this mid-term election will either secure a path forward to reclaim America's core conservative values or it will give the President and the Progressive Democrats carte blanche to finish their job of taking the world's most powerful country on an orgiastic spending binge, destroying America's financial future. We must not forget that the REAL immediate power lies in the House and Senate. At this point in time, winning the presidency is of lesser importance to the future of the Republican Party than are all the House and Senate seats up for grabs in 2014.

Win THEM and we will be better positioned to win the big one.

Chapter 15

Doing the math...to WIN

How Republicans can win in a changing America

Republican strategists from around the country...

have looked at the chart in this chapter which shows the voting data from the individual U.S. states during the 2012 Presidential election. Many of them have probably come to the conclusion that Republicans have a long way to go to defeat the Democrats in Democrat strongholds or in 'Purple' or swing states.

These experts may be right about the degree of difficulty, but a win is far from impossible. To win the Presidency in the U.S. election system, a candidate must win 270 electoral votes from the states. Many myopic Republicans, when expressing their preference for a 2016 candidate, are simply unable to discuss how to get those 270 electoral votes from the states to win! Dreams do not win elections, and there is no second place trophy in American politics.

Both Republicans and Democrats have vulnerabilities. Here are a few of them:

Losing states with under 15% winning margins of victory

Rs: If we take states where the Republicans only had a 15% or less margin of victory (Alaska 14% 3 votes, Arizona 10.1% 11 votes, Georgia 8% 16 votes, Indiana 10.5% 11 votes, Mississippi 12% 6 votes, Missouri 9.6% 10 votes, Montana 13.5% 3 votes, North Carolina 2.2% 15 votes, South Carolina 10.6% 9 votes) we can see that those states, while appearing safe, need shoring up before the next election otherwise the Republican candidate could end up with <u>a loss of 84 electoral votes from their total of 206 votes won in the 2012 election, leaving them with only 122 electoral votes!</u>

188

Ds: If the Democrats were to lose states where they had a 15% or less margin of victory like: Colorado 4.7% 9 votes, Florida 0.9% 29 votes, Iowa 5.6% 6 votes, Michigan 9.5% 16 votes, Minnesota 7.7% 10 votes, Nevada 6.6% 6 votes, New Hampshire 5.8% 4 votes, New Mexico 9.9% 5 votes, Ohio 1.9% 18 votes, Oregon 11.8% 7 votes, Pennsylvania 5.2% 20 votes, Virginia 3.0% 13 votes, Washington 14.1% 12 votes and Wisconsin 6.7% 10 votes, they would end up with <u>a loss of 165 electoral votes from their total of 332 votes won in the 2012 election, leaving the Ds with only 167 electoral votes!</u>

Possible Republican losses = 84 vote vulnerability
Possible Democrat losses = 165 vote vulnerability

Losing states with under 10% winning margins of victory

Rs: Republicans could be vulnerable in those states where the Republican winning margin was under 10%: Georgia 8.0% 16 votes, Missouri 9.6% 10 votes and North Carolina 2.2% 15 votes. Losing these states would be <u>a loss of 41 electoral votes</u>.

Ds: Using the same 10% or under figure, the Democrats could be vulnerable in Colorado 4.7% 9 votes, Florida 0.9% 29 votes, Iowa 5.6% 6 votes, Michigan 9.5% 16 votes, Minnesota 7.7% 10 votes, Nevada 6.6% 6 votes, New Hampshire 5.8% 4 votes, New Mexico 9.9% 5 votes, Ohio 1.9% 18 votes, Pennsylvania 5.2% 20 votes, Virginia 3.0% 13 votes and Wisconsin 6.7% 10 votes. A loss in all of these states would be <u>a loss of 146 electoral votes</u>.

Possible Republican losses = 41 vote vulnerability
Possible Democrat losses = 146 vote vulnerability

Losing states with under 6% winning margins of victory

Rs: Republicans are only vulnerable in the State of North Carolina (2.2%) which would <u>lose them 15 electoral votes</u>.

Ds: Democrats are vulnerable in Colorado 4.7% 9 votes, Florida 0.9% 29 votes, Iowa 5.6% 6 votes, New Hampshire 5.8% 4 votes, Ohio 1.9% 18 votes, Pennsylvania 5.2% 20 votes, and Virginia 3.9% 13 votes. If they lost them all, they would <u>lose a total of 99 electoral votes</u>.

Possible Republican losses = 15 vote vulnerability
Possible Democrat losses = 99 vote vulnerability

The adjusted bases of the Rs and Ds

The massive wins for the Democrats in traditional Democrat strongholds with margins of victory over 15% would give the Democrats a base of 167 certain electoral votes. For the Republicans, the figure is 122 electoral votes for states with margins of victory over 15%.

Adjusted R base = 122 electoral votes
Adjusted D base = 167 electoral votes

Adjusted R Base plus wins of all D states with under 10% marginal wins equals defeat

If the Republicans picked off all Blue states where the Democrat winning margin was 10% or less, they would gain 146 electoral votes, and when added to their base of 122 votes would give them 268 electoral votes - not enough to win. That's why Republicans must also concentrate on the tougher wins, the states where Democrats enjoy BETWEEN 10-15% dominance.

How Republicans can win in a changing America

Two of those states might be Oregon (7 votes won by 11.8%) or Washington (12 votes won by 14.1%) either one of which, when added to Rs' base (122) plus their capture of all states won by the Democrats with winning margins under 10% (146) would put the Rs over the top (with Oregon by 5 votes or with Washington by 10 votes).

Another strategy for the Republicans might be the longest of long shots...trying to capture all 15% or less Democrat marginal win states PLUS a state or two with big electoral votes that might be won by targeting specific voter groups. They are long shots because they include: California (21% marginal win), Illinois (16.2% marginal win), and New York (26.6% marginal win).

Five pathways to a Republican victory in 2016

Scenario 1: Pathway to 305 Electoral Votes

All Republican 2012 electoral vote wins (206) including North Carolina plus all under-6% marginal Democrat electoral vote wins (99)

Republicans keep all the states they won in the 2012 election in their column, totaling 206. To that they pick off all the states where the Democrats won with an under-6% majority: Colorado 4.7% 9 votes, Florida 0.9% 29 votes, Iowa 5.6% 6 votes, New Hampshire 5.8% 4 votes, Ohio 1.9% 18 votes, Pennsylvania 5.2% 20 votes and Virginia 3.0% 13 votes. That would give them 305 electoral votes, 35 more than they need to win.

Scenario 2: Pathway to 275 or 277 Electoral Votes

All Republican 2012 electoral vote wins (206) including North Carolina plus all under-5% marginal Democrat electoral vote wins (69 w/OH or 71 w/PA)

Republicans keep all the states they won in the 2012 election in their column, totaling 206. To that they pick off Colorado 4.7% 9 votes, Florida 0.9% 29 votes, Ohio 1.9% 18 votes and Virginia 3.0% 13 votes. This would give them 275 electoral votes, five more than needed to win.

If they didn't get Ohio but got Pennsylvania instead, they would end up with 277 total electoral votes. *If they got both, they would end up with 295 electoral votes.*

Scenario 3: Pathway to 275 Electoral Votes

All Republican 2012 electoral vote wins (206) including North Carolina plus all under-2% marginal Democrat electoral vote wins and two swing states

Republicans keep all the states they won in the 2012 election in their column, totaling 206. To that they pick off both of the under-2% Democrat majority win states: Florida 0.9% 29 votes and Ohio 1.9% 18 votes. This would give them 253. Add two swing states like Colorado 4.7% 9 votes and Virginia 3.0% 13 votes and the number becomes 275, five more electoral votes than needed to win.

Scenario 4: Pathway to 290 Electoral Votes

All Republican 2012 electoral vote wins (206) minus North Carolina (15) plus all under-6% marginal Democrat electoral vote wins (99)

If the Republicans lost North Carolina (which they only won by 2.2% in the last election) they would lose 15 electoral votes. Hanging on to all the other votes they won in other states by safe margins would put them at 191 electoral votes. If the Republicans were successful in winning all the Democrat-leaning states mentioned in Scenario 2 - the under 5% - (69 votes) but lost North Carolina, they would have only 260 votes and lose.

However, if the Republicans were successful in winning all the *under-6%* Democrat marginal win states as mentioned in Scenario 1 (99 votes) while still losing North Carolina, they would still win big with 290 electoral votes.

Scenario 5: Pathway to 270 Electoral Votes

All Republican 2012 electoral vote wins (206) minus North Carolina (15) plus all under-5% marginal Democrat electoral vote wins plus one 10 electoral vote state

The Republicans hold all their states except North Carolina and start with 191 votes. They are only successful in picking off the under-5% Democrat marginal win states: Colorado 4.7% 9 votes, Florida 0.9% 29 votes, Ohio 1.9% 18 votes and Virginia 3.0% 13 votes. They would lose because they would only end up with 260 electoral votes.

Republicans could turn it around, however, if they added a state like Wisconsin 6.7% 10 votes or Minnesota 7.7% 10 votes. Then they would win with 270 electoral votes.

One thing is for certain, no matter which election scenario the Republicans choose in 2016, the road to 270 votes will be long and the victory will be a hard-fought one.

State Populations (2010 U.S. Census) Voting Statistics (Associated Press)

State	Pop. Change 2000 to 2010	Red or Blue State in 2012 Election		Electoral Votes	% difference
Alabama	+ 7.5 %	Red		9	22.3 R
Alaska	+ 13.3 %	Red		3	14.0 R
Arizona	+ 24.6 %	Red		11	10.1 R
Arkansas	+ 9.1 %	Red		6	23.6 R
California	+ 10.0 %		Blue	55	21.0 B
Colorado	+ 16.9 %		Blue	9	4.7 B
Connecticut	+ 4.9 %		Blue	7	18.0 B
Delaware	+ 14.6 %		Blue	3	18.6 B
District of Columbia	+ 5.2 %		Blue	3	84.3 B
Florida	+ 17.6 %		Blue	29	0.9 B
Georgia	+ 18.3 %	Red		16	8.0 R
Hawaii	+ 12.3 %		Blue	4	42.8 B
Idaho	+ 21.1 %	Red		4	31.9 R
Illinois	+ 3.3 %		Blue	20	16.2 B
Indiana	+ 6.6 %	Red		11	10.5 R
Iowa	+ 4.1 %		Blue	6	5.6 B
Kansas	+ 6.1 %	Red		6	22.2 R
Kentucky	+ 7.4 %	Red		8	22.7 R
Louisiana	+ 1.4 %	Red		8	17.2 R
Maine	+ 4.2 %		Blue	4	15.1 B
Maryland	+ 9.0 %		Blue	10	25.1 B
Massachusetts	+ 3.1 %		Blue	11	23.2 B
Michigan	- 0.6 %		Blue	16	9.5 B
Minnesota	+ 7.8 %		Blue	10	7.7 B
Mississippi	+ 4.3 %	Red		6	12.0 R
Missouri	+ 7.0 %	Red		10	9.6 R
Montana	+ 9.7 %	Red		3	13.5 R
Nebraska	+ 6.7 %	Red		5	22.7 R
Nevada	+ 35.1 %		Blue	6	6.6 B
New Hampshire	+ 6.5 %		Blue	4	5.8 B
New Jersey	+ 4.5 %		Blue	14	17.1 B
New Mexico	+ 13.2 %		Blue	5	9.9 B
New York	+ 2.1 %		Blue	29	26.6 B
North Carolina	+ 18.5 %	Red		15	2.2 R
North Dakota	+ 4.7 %	Red		3	19.8 R
Ohio	+ 1.6 %		Blue	18	1.9 B
Oklahoma	+ 8.7 %	Red		7	33.6 R
Oregon	+ 12.0 %		Blue	7	11.8 B
Pennsylvania	+ 3.4 %		Blue	20	5.2 B
Rhode Island	+ 0.4 %		Blue	4	27.2 B
South Carolina	+ 15.3 %	Red		9	10.6 R
South Dakota	+ 7.9 %	Red		3	18.0 R
Tennessee	+ 11.5 %	Red		11	20.5 R
Texas	+ 20.6 %	Red		38	15.8 R
Utah	+ 23.8 %	Red		6	47.9 R
Vermont	+ 2.8 %		Blue	3	35.8 B
Virginia	+ 13.0 %		Blue	13	3.0 B
Washington	+ 14.1 %		Blue	12	14.1 B
West Virginia	+ 2.5 %	Red		5	26.8 R
Wisconsin	+ 6.0 %		Blue	10	6.7 B
Wyoming	+ 14.1 %	Red		3	41.3 R

How Republicans can win in a changing America

Chapter 16

The Third Way

How Republicans can win in a changing America

The Third Way

(Def. a political ideology that seeks to combine egalitarian and individualist policies and elements of socialism and capitalism).

Most of us associate the *Third Way*, with the rise of former Prime Minister of the U.K., Tony Blair, who was gingerly feeling his way forward after the Thatcher years. England was looking for a middle ground, some form of governance and an economic system that was in equilibrium with each other after Margaret Thatcher swung the pendulum to the right of England's political center to correct for decades of left-wing Labour-dominated governance since WWII.

Blair based his political future on the Third Way as a means to unite opposing political and economic forces and form a more cohesive and powerful consensus by appealing to the essential reasonableness and 'Britishness' of his citizens.

Not to be outdone, the 'Comeback Kid,' Bill Clinton, embraced the philosophy as one America could use, but because he had neither the opportunity nor power to do so, he could only give it lip service.

The Republicans' Third Way

Much is being made in the press about the so-called 'feuding' between Senator Rand Paul of Kentucky and Governor Chris Christie of New Jersey, each one being fashioned by the national press as representing the bipolar aspects of the GOP and inferring slight hope for victory. Their reports require a suspension of belief that the search is still on for the Republican candidate that can win.

The contest has not even begun yet the press expects us to believe that the primaries are over, the dust has settled, and the two polar opposite factions represent the only surviving powerful forces in the Republican Party.

This is just the media's sleight of hand, allowing us to fall asleep at the wheel by stoking the fires of controversy about the 'schism' within the Republican Party. As with most things, there's an element of truth, albeit tiny, in the feud.

<u>There are divergent voices representing opposing points of view within the Party, but these are not the only two.</u>

What IS new are the choices both men seem to represent and offer. One is absolute freedom with absolute loyalty to the Constitution with an absolute pledge to scale down, cut back and stifle the growth of the Federal government. The other is a 'whatever works,' pragmatic, non-ideological approach to problem-solving delivered up with a head butt or blow to the solar plexus.

<u>Republicans cannot win by choosing the extremes of a laissez-faire Doctor Spock or an *in-your-face* Tony Soprano to be the Party's standard-bearer.</u>

They want and need...a Third Way.

The Republicans' Third Way is first a place of policy and then a person. It is an amalgamation of political positions that have been widely discussed, debated and agreed upon, within the Party. These are positions that do not stray too far from the Republicans' core values, but represent negotiating buoys that send a signal to independents and moderate Democrats that the Republicans are less intransigent than they were led to believe.

198

Questions 26-27 (GOVERNMENT ROLE) COMBINED RESPONSES *

	"pure liberal"	"populist"	"libertarian"	"pure conservative"	undesignated
2013 Sep 5-8	23	16	22	28	11
2012 Sep 24-27	24	14	25	27	11
2011 Sep 8-11	18	19	26	27	10
2010 Sep 13-16	19	16	23	33	10
2010 Jun 11-13	21	16	23	27	13
2009 Aug 31-Sep 2	18	19	23	31	9
2008 Sep 8-11	23	17	23	29	9
2007 Sep 14-16	20	20	21	26	13
2006 Sep 7-10	21	20	21	25	12
2005 Sep 12-15	24	19	21	27	9
2004 Nov 19-21	16	19	23	30	12
2004 Sep 13-15	20	20	17	29	14
2003 Sep 8-10	19	22	19	31	9
2002 Sep 5-8	18	23	19	29	11
2001 Oct 5-6	18	30	17	23	12
2001 Sep 7-10	16	18	22	30	14
2000 Sep 11-13	16	18	18	30	18
1999 Sep 10-14	15	23	23	31	8
1998 Oct 29-30	14	23	19	29	15
1998 Apr 17-19	13	17	21	34	15
1997 Jan 31-Feb 2	13	17	24	31	15
1996 Jan 12-15	13	20	20	35	12
1994 Nov 2-6	15	20	20	32	13

199

How Republicans can win in a changing America

GALLUP POLL SOCIAL SERIES: GOVERNANCE

Questions 26-27 (GOVERNMENT ROLE) COMBINED RESPONSES *

	"pure liberal"	"populist"	"libertarian"	"pure conservative"	undesignated
1994 Oct 22-25	16	19	21	33	11
1994 Jan 15-17	16	20	22	30	14
1993 Dec 17-19	13	23	22	31	11
1993 Apr 22-24	17	25	20	27	11
1993 Mar 22-24	20	27	19	24	10

Note: "Pure liberals" are defined as those who want government to do more to solve country's problems but not promote traditional values.

"Populists" are defined as those who want government to do more to solve the country's problems and to promote traditional values.

"Libertarians" are defined as those who think the government is doing too much to solve the country's problems and do not think the government should promote traditional values.

"Pure conservatives" are defined as those who think the government is doing too much to solve the country's problems but want the government to promote traditional values.

* Questions asked: Q1. Some people think the government is trying to do too many things that should be left to individuals and businesses. Others think that government should do more to solve our country's problems. Which comes closer to your own view? Q2. Some people think the government should promote traditional values in our society. Others think the government should not favor any particular set of values. Which comes closer to your own view?

Authors' note: Respondents answered the questions by self-identifying as one of the above-mentioned five groups

How Republicans can win in a changing America

The previous chart was compiled from data gathered by the Gallup polling organization and is reprinted here with their permission.

It reveals, over a 20-year period, how the American electorate has identified itself with cultural change and how it views the role of government in its lives. Even though this is a simplified measurement of two of the main public policy directions, it points the way to how complex the public policy debates *are* in campaigns.

It also represents a warning to Republicans: should they not attempt to find a *third way* candidate to run in the 2016 Presidential Election they will lose.

The reasons are: the Liberals are maintaining unwavering strength and the Democratic Party knows how to split off *Libertarians* and *Populists* with adroit messaging (on selected issues) while at the same time demonizing Republican candidates with targeted rhetoric. This was clearly evident in the recent Presidential Election of 2012.

While the above political identifiers used by Gallup were instructive, we believe that they can be further defined to illustrate the current attitudes of the electorate on issues of *cultural change* and *role of government*. The findings of September 2013 revealed the true issue-driven structure of the American electorate, and we have decided to re-label them, accordingly:

Liberal-Progressives = 23%
Safety-net Populists = 16%
Economic Conservatives = 22%
Social Conservatives = 28%
and Unknown/Mixed = 11%

How Republicans can win in a changing America

A noticeable shift has occurred over the last ten years in two specific categories: the Liberal-Progressives have increased from 19% to 23% and the Safety-net Populists have declined from 22% to 16% of the total electorate. It should be pointed out that the percentage of Economic and Social Conservatives has essentially remained unchanged, 22% and 28%, respectively, over the last ten years.

Candidate Romney lost because his campaign concentrated too much on obliging the Social Conservatives and spent too much of his time on economic messages. His campaign offered little or nothing to the Safety-net Populists.

A winning strategy would have been to win 90% or more of the Social Conservatives (SO-CONS), 75% of the Economic Conservatives (ECO-CONS) and at least break even (50/50) with the Safety-net Populists (POPULISTS). This, we believe, is the winning formula for the third way candidate...

.90 SO-CONS + .75 ECO-CONS + .50 POPULISTS = 52% WIN

Previous Third Ways

Dwight Eisenhower emerged as the Third Way candidate in 1952 from the feud between the insiders represented by Thomas Dewey and Robert Taft, both who could not win on their own. Later, it was Ronald Reagan who became the Third Way after factions supporting George H.W. Bush and John Connally realized neither could win on their own.

Now it's time for a new Third Way discussion and search, one that must discover another outsider who can change the landlocked polarity in WASHDC. It has been done before, and it is time to do it again. It just takes common sense and uncommon courage.

202

The Third Way will be the blueprint for the new Republican Creed going forward into the 2014 and 2016 elections AND it will help decide who the Rs' next Presidential candidate will be. In short, the Third Way will lead to the Third Man (or Woman) who will represent the new *re-united* Republican Party. This can only happen after the GOP has done a self-administered much-needed intervention and walked the hot coals of the divisive intraparty issues that have kept it from finding its new Reagan for the last twenty-five years.

The Reagan Era of the 80s is officially over as are (for the most part) the Cultural Wars that began in the 1960s. Even the Republican National Committee in their "Republican Strategy Survey for 2014" posed a question to all its members, "Do you believe the Republican Party should continue to embrace social issues or are these too divisive when it comes to winning elections?" Their response categories were either 'to embrace' or 'too divisive.' This seems to show that the issue is being vetted at all levels of the Party, already, and signals a possible change of priorities.

The *new improved Republican Party* will be stronger for the effort as its whole will now truly equal the sum of its divergent parts. It will have a renewed sense of purpose, a new unmistakable direction and be able to play political 'change-up ball' with opponents who literally invented the game.

The successful candidate will most certainly come from one of the five Presidential leader groups mentioned in Chapter 6: *The Great Manager, The Problem-Solver, The Super Politician, The Caretaker or The White Knight.*

Whichever mantle the candidate assumes, he will need to fit the following 'Help Wanted' job description:

203

1. "Wanted: One top <u>manager</u> with extensive experience in small-to-large business(es) preferably in a senior leadership position with direct responsibility for the motivation of employees of diverse backgrounds and skill-sets.

2. Must have a proven track record of diplomacy and time-tested communication skills and be bi-lingual (preferably Spanish). Individual must have lived and/or worked overseas, been responsible for budgets of upwards of $100 million and be able to manage approx. 2.6 million federal workers (85% of which live outside the Nation's Capital).

3. The ideal candidate must be in excellent physical and mental health, have a clear vision for America and an identifiable ideology, be able to articulate it <u>and</u> be able to compromise for the good of the country AND be a good listener to advisors with superior issue-specific knowledge.

4. In addition, the candidate must have been *unsuccessful* at realizing some of his goals during his formative years and have learned from his mistakes and be able to apply that knowledge to new tasks.

5. Subject must possess a good sense of humor, a winning smile, be affable, suffer fools gladly and be willing to make friends for America without apologizing for its values.

6. A thorough understanding of economics, world geography, history, political science and psychology are crucial as is a deeply rooted appreciation for America's core values, its religious beliefs, its Constitution and Bill of Rights.

7. As a consequence of the job, applicant must be willing to undertake extensive domestic and foreign travel.

How Republicans can win in a changing America

8. The successful applicant must have been or be married and have been faithful to his spouse (children are optional, but will be scored as a plus given the value of the parenting experience).

9. Prior service in the military is highly desirable as is knowledge of the country's Status of Forces Agreements, strategic basing objectives and international agreements with organizations like the U.N. and NATO.

10. The candidate must be willing to secure America's borders to stem the flow of illegal aliens, but also be willing to engage the country in an open and honest dialogue about reforming its immigration policy. (He must realize that America's immigrants are an integral part of our nation and one that continues to make the USA the most successful nation in modern history.)

11. Subject is not required to be able to play golf, basketball, touch football, soccer, badminton, go wind-surfing, yachting or play other sports, but must be willing to ceremoniously open major contests for each if asked.

12. Knowledge of the country's energy demands and resources along with new renewable energy technologies will be helpful. Candidate must be able to stand for long periods of time, occasionally with hand over heart and be able to recite the Pledge of Allegiance and know the words to the national anthem.

13. Subject must know what the national motto is and be able to name the capitals of all U.S. States (and know how many there are).

14. The successful applicant must have strong spiritual and/or religious convictions as they are important to the majority of the Nation's citizens.

15. Finally, the winning candidate must know the difference between right and wrong and have a steadfast belief in the inherent goodness of his/her fellow man while recognizing that evil is not a concept but a reality to be reckoned with."

Finding the *better candidate*, not the *perfect* candidate, is the key. Winning is winning, and losing is losing, period. Republicans must set the bar high. If we don't, we will not be honoring the highest office in the land and do ourselves and our country a disservice. To paraphrase Horace Greely's advice in the mid-19th century to, "Go West young man, go West," we say, "Go outside, Republicans. Go outside." The GOP did in 1952 and in 1980, and look what happened.

The Third Way is the only way Republicans can win in a changing America.

POSTSCRIPT

The best offense is a good offense.

The last thing we need is more acrimony in our politics, but we must resign ourselves to its inevitability. There are more financial cliffs and other confrontations looming on the horizon, too. That's why Republicans must dig in, stick to their principles, and tough it out.

If the President keeps insisting on tax hikes every time the Republicans present a budget and refuses to back down from his promise to veto any bill that doesn't contain tax hikes on the latest rich group of high income earners, then the Republicans should simply say, "Mr. President, good luck. You broke it, and now you've bought it. Welcome to your legacy. We don't need more of your ultra-progressive ideology to infiltrate the body politic of our appropriations committees or keep us from achieving real meaningful tax reform."

There is too much taxation without representation already without greasing the slippery slope that would ensure more social engineering through Progressive tax policy. The paltry billions that even a 100% wealth confiscation tax on the rich would raise would only be enough money to fund eight days of government programs and services!

His 'us versus them' war on success is the worst kind of pandering and should be called by its real name, a pure ideological money grab. Republicans need to be repeating their message for revising the tax code...for everybody's benefit. Then there's Obamacare and immigration reform. While many believe that we have gone too far down the Obamacare road to turn back, turn back we must.

That which man has irresponsibly cobbled together can also be dismantled. The question is how?

Should Republicans introduce legislation that amends aspects of Obamacare so this financial colossus never sees the light of day in its present form or should they delay funding or deny it altogether? They must be aware of the inherent dangers in a 'deny or delay' strategy as the Administration is particularly adept at demonizing honest opposition.

One thing they MUST do, however, is continue telling the story of the roughshod and underhanded way the bill was passed and keep reminding the American public that legislative tyranny is not compromise. Republicans must keep throwing this up in the Democrats' faces while characterizing their tactics as being fundamentally unfair to Americans of both parties.

Pure obstructionist politics, like trying to shut down the government and endless 'stop Obamacare' votes in the House will not win enough of the *right voters* to the Republican side on this issue or any other.

Immigration reform, however, may be the one area where the Legislative Branch can actually win back some favorability among the electorate, that is if they don't reward illegal residents with an all-encompassing 'hall pass' or get bogged down in procedural bickering OR start fighting over the minutia of the legislation before they've even had meaningful public discussions with their constituents. There will be plenty of issues to wrangle over during the next three years. The real question becomes: are politicians of both parties ready to compromise or are we stuck in a vicious cycle of constant power shifting from one party to the other until American voters simply tune out and turn off in massive numbers?

We would like to leave you with what we believe is the central argument that overarches and influences all the others. It is the core argument of our present political time in history. While it's been played out in other societies and countries during the last few centuries, it's not had its day here... yet. It is:

How to balance the rights of the individual with the needs of the nation

The two are not mutually exclusive, and it is THIS argument that undergirds every single political argument on every single political issue facing us, much more than a simple *small vs. big government* ideology. We have a fundamental philosophical divide that must be addressed and bridged soon or we are surely doomed to a future of perennial power-shifting and a gradual decline of our fidelity to truth, fairness, our institutions and our entire political system.

Ignoring it or pretending that it's a temporary condition that will take care of itself over time, won't cut it. Republicans must step up, internally, and make their argument with their peers and see how it relates to every single one of their platform issues. Then they must craft an entirely new, unambiguous policy document that addresses how each issue relates to and balances the rights of the individual with those of the nation.

Neither individuals' rights nor the integrity of our Nation's should be left out of the equation. If one trumps the other totally then both become vulnerable and subject to the oppression of whichever ideology is embraced by the power structure. As we see it, there are only two courses of action for any individual or group that sees itself as irrelevant, ignored or unwanted.

How Republicans can win in a changing America

One is to cancel our membership in society by not voting or participating, and the other is to protest. We cannot afford either one. Our mantra must be:

Many voices, many choices. Many choices, many possibilities. Many possibilities, many opportunities...for all.

As the traditional champions of individuals' rights, Republicans need to take the first steps, now.

They must sweep away the confusion that exists with their Party's positions on the issues facing our country AND they must make the individual/nation connections to those positions, clearly and earnestly. They must reject the small (or limited) government vs. big government stance. That is a Trojan Horse for the real argument: the case for *efficient/fair government vs. undemocratic power-driven government.*

On an individual level, we must not ignore any attempt by Government to eliminate or subordinate our personal freedoms or replace them entirely using explanations like, "we do this for the greater good of our country" ('the 99% excuse'). When we are confronted with this same rationale by colleagues, friends or families in seemingly innocent conversations, we must not bite our lip and just *go along to get along*, for there is a price to be paid for silence. It is the impression by others that we agree with them.

We Republicans cannot falter, cannot demur, but neither can we afford to appear overly-aggressive, because the left will surely use our passion against us, painting us as zealots, radicals or out-of-control anti-social bullies. That's why we must use our intensity wisely, carefully channeling it, always towards the subject (the conversation) not the object (the conversation partner).

How Republicans can win in a changing America

Over-factualizing and filibustering will not succeed. We will only win by linking every issue to the core argument...<u>by protecting and preserving individuals' rights, we protect those of the community and the Nation!</u>

If there ever were a time for honest forthright speech that consistently makes those connections, it is now when it can still be debated, before the elections of 2014 and 2016.

Despite America's apparent impatience with details, we are convinced that voters are now ready for and want the truth (even the details) about issues they hold dear. The party that gets *and holds* the voters' attention and makes its argument with sincerity, clarity, passion and tolerance <u>will win the next election.</u>

Thankfully, we are still a nation of patriots and reasonable men and women.

211

ABOUT THE AUTHORS

Lance Tarrance is an award-winning political strategist and Republican pollster who has conducted hundreds of polls for many of America's leading corporations and elected leaders. He was a senior strategist to Senator John McCain's presidential campaign and was involved in the campaigns of Barry Goldwater, Richard Nixon, Ronald Reagan, Jack Kemp and George W. Bush. He founded and managed Tarrance and Associates for ten years and then, after merging his company with Gallup, served on its Board of Directors for five years, later becoming the first  Managing Partner of Gallup China in Beijing. He has authored two previous books on political polling. In April of 2013 he was inducted into the Association of Political Consultants' Hall of Fame for his outstanding contributions. He now calls Santa Fe, home.

 Stephan Helgesen is a retired career Foreign Service Officer. He lived and worked in over 25 countries over a 30 year period and served under thirteen different U.S. Ambassadors in Europe, the Caribbean Basin and the Pacific Rim during the Reagan, Bush, Clinton and Bush administrations. In 2006, he was appointed by New Mexico's Governor to head up that state's Office of Science and Technology, a position he held for nearly four years. He has authored three previous books, written hundreds of articles on politics, economics and social issues and managed the campaign of a Republican Lt. Governor candidate. He lives in the mountains outside Albuquerque, New Mexico.

How Republicans can win in a changing America

Made in the USA
Middletown, DE
09 June 2015